Supporting English Language Learners in Math Class

Grades K-2

Rusty Bresser
Kathy Melanese
Christine Sphar

Math Solutions Publications
Sausalito, CA

To all English language learners . . .

*We appreciate the linguistic and cultural diversity
that they bring to our classrooms and are grateful
to their teachers for welcoming them
with high expectations and support.*

Math Solutions Publications
150 Gate 5 Road
Sausalito, CA 94965
www.mathsolutions.com

The publisher would like to acknowledge material adapted from the following sources:

Pages 40 and 43: Illustrations adapted from *Math By All Means: Geometry, Grades 1–2* by Chris Confer. © 1994 Math Solutions Publications.
Pages 95 and 96: Illustrations adapted from *Minilessons for Math Practice, Grades K–2* by Rusty Bresser and Caren Holtzman. © 2006 Math Solutions Publications.
Page 112: Chapter 7, "Junk Sorting," adapted from *About Teaching Mathematics: A K–8 Resource, Third Edition* by Marilyn Burns, © 2007 Math Solutions Publications, and from "All Sorts of Logic" by Frank Threewit from *ComMuniCator* 31 (2), © 2006 California Mathematics Council.
Pages 190 and 192: "Trade Up for a Nickel Game Board" and "Trade Up for a Dime Game Board" Blackline Masters adapted from an activity created by Elisabeth Frausto.

Library of Congress Cataloging-in-Publication Data

Bresser, Rusty.
  Supporting English language learners in math class, grades K/2 / Rusty Bresser, Kathy Melanese, Christine Sphar.
      p. cm.
  Includes bibliographical references and index.
  ISBN 978-0-941355-84-1 (alk. paper)
  1. Mathematics—Study and teaching (Elementary) 2. English language—Study and teaching (Elementary)—Foreign speakers. I. Melanese, Kathy. II. Sphar, Christine. III. Title.
  QA135.6.B7349 2008
  372.7—dc22
                                 2008021365

Editor: Toby Gordon
Production: Melissa L. Inglis-Elliott
Cover design: Jan Streitburger
Interior design: Joni Doherty
Composition: ICC Macmillan Inc.

Printed in the United States of America on acid-free paper
12 11 10 09 08   ML   1 2 3 4 5

A Message from Marilyn Burns

We at Math Solutions Professional Development believe that teaching math well calls for increasing our understanding of the math we teach, seeking deeper insights into how children learn mathematics, and refining our lessons to best promote students' learning.

Math Solutions Publications shares classroom-tested lessons and teaching expertise from our faculty of Math Solutions Inservice instructors as well as from other respected math educators. Our publications are part of the nationwide effort we've made since 1984 that now includes

- more than five hundred face-to-face inservice programs each year for teachers and administrators in districts across the country;
- annually publishing professional development books, now totaling more than seventy titles and spanning the teaching of all math topics in kindergarten through grade 8;
- four series of videos for teachers, plus a video for parents, that show math lessons taught in actual classrooms;
- on-site visits to schools to help refine teaching strategies and assess student learning; and
- free online support, including grade-level lessons, book reviews, inservice information, and district feedback, all in our quarterly *Math Solutions Online Newsletter*.

For information about all of the products and services we have available, please visit our website at *www.mathsolutions.com*. You can also contact us to discuss math professional development needs by calling (800) 868-9092 or by sending an email to *info@mathsolutions.com*.

We're always eager for your feedback and interested in learning about your particular needs. We look forward to hearing from you.

Math Solutions.
PUBLICATIONS

Contents

Foreword

Writing this book began with our conviction that communication is key to the teaching and learning of mathematics. Communication involves talking, listening, reading, writing, demonstrating, and observing. It means participating in social interaction, sharing thoughts with others, and listening to others share their ideas.

Communication helps children construct understandings of mathematical ideas and develop connections between their informal knowledge and the abstract symbolism of mathematical concepts. Communication makes mathematical thinking observable, thus making mathematical talk critical to the assessment process and to learning itself. Teachers find out what students understand or are confused about by listening to their ideas. And communication encourages students to reflect on their own knowledge and can help students clarify their ideas or change their thinking, especially when they hear others' points of view. Communicating about mathematical ideas is therefore important to both the teacher and the student.

While communication is important to mathematical learning, it can also increase inequity for English language learners (ELLs). If math instruction and modes of communication are in English, students who are English language learners may not have equal access to classroom discussions unless teachers provide extra support. The equity principle in *Principles and Standards for School Mathematics* (NCTM 2000) states that all students, regardless of their personal characteristics, backgrounds, or physical challenges, must have opportunities to study and learn mathematics.

Equity in math instruction does not simply mean that everyone receives the same math lesson. Equity means that English language learners deserve the opportunity to be as successful as their peers who grew up speaking English. For many English language learners, especially those not given a chance to learn in their primary language, the assumption has existed that they will acquire English just through immersion in an English-speaking classroom. Likewise, ELLs are expected to learn math content just by being present for the math lessons. Ignoring the role of student participation and communication in math lessons can lead to inequity in the education of this population.

This is not to say that ELLs aren't as capable as their peers or are somehow lacking in what is needed to achieve in school. Students who speak another language bring a unique linguistic experience with them to school. Many times it is just a language barrier that prevents them from demonstrating the depth of their understanding of the content presented. They are in no way deficient. In fact, the opposite is true. They bring the diverse cultural traditions of their home with them to school and help educate us about acceptance, tolerance, and respect of differences.

The language of instruction is transparent to teachers who are native English speakers. Not so for English language learners. English, as all languages, has a complex structure that native speakers begin learning early in life and later use effortlessly and automatically. Our hope is, with this book, you will see some of the hidden pieces of language that seem so obvious to those of us who speak English as a native language. By providing your students with ongoing explicit language instruction, even during math, you are giving them an opportunity to learn both English and content matter. Language and thought are connected; we can't have one without the other. And thinking is what we hope to facilitate with each math lesson. Therefore, in order to provide an equitable education for our ELLs, we are obligated to recognize their needs and make modifications in our instruction in order to provide the richest experiences in education for all students. Our interest in designing those modifications to support teachers is what led us to write this book.

Working with English language learners, while rewarding, is not easy. The fact that teachers conduct their instruction in a language that some students do not yet use fluently forces teachers to rethink the most basic element of their work, the medium of instruction. Many politicians are ready to point fingers at teachers for the gap in achievement between English language learners and their native English-speaking peers. But few of these critics are ready with concrete suggestions as to how to modify the very medium of instruction in order to improve the success of ELLs. As teachers ourselves, we know that time is one of the most valuable commodities in education. Adding a curricular goal, namely

English language development, only puts more demands on instructional time. When designing the lesson modifications proposed in this book, we sought to find ways in which math content goals and language development goals could be met at the same time. We also held to the philosophy that the best intervention is effective first teaching. By actively involving English language learners in math lessons *and* in language development simultaneously, we increase the learning that takes place in each and every lesson and reduce the amount of time needed to provide individualized or small-group instruction. Language development will always take time; we offer suggestions to make sure it's time well spent.

As teachers, as university faculty, and as instructional coaches, we collaborated over lesson plans, in the classroom and at the computer, to create a resource that would promote communication in the instruction of mathematics, provide equity for students learning in their second language, and support teachers in accomplishing the goals of content instruction and language development.

Acknowledgments

We'd like to thank the following people for making this book possible: Toby Gordon and Joan Carlson for their editorial expertise; Melissa L. Inglis-Elliott for her work on the book's production; Marilyn Burns for her support; and Susana Dutro and the California Reading and Literature Project for their groundbreaking work with English language learners.

We'd like to thank the following principals and teachers for allowing us to work at their schools and in their classrooms: from Lexington Elementary School, El Cajon, CA: Principal Sylvia Casas-Werkman, Cynthia Cox, Mary Najera, and Judy Fossgreen; from Lincoln Acres Elementary School, National City, CA: Principal Deborah Costa Hernandez, Kristin Burer; from Jackson Elementary School, San Diego, CA: Principal Rupi Boyd, Sharon Fargason, and Alison Williams; from Palmer Way Elementary School, National City, CA: Principal Richard Hanks, Diana Whitaker; from McKinley Elementary School, San Diego, CA: Principal Julie Ashton-Gray, Danielle Pickett; from Florence Elementary School, San Diego, CA: Principal Mary Estil, Elisabeth Frausto, and Frannie McKenzie; from Freese Elementary School, San Diego, CA: Principal Midge Backensto, Shawn Yoshimoto; from Webster Elementary School, San Diego, CA: Principal Jennifer White, Amy Vadagama.

Christine Sphar would like to thank her parents for their support, her husband for his patience, the wonderful children and teachers of Lexington Elementary for their vitality, and her coauthors for their professional curiosity and work ethic.

Rusty Bresser would like to thank his coauthors for their creative collaboration and for sharing their wisdom about English language development. And as always, gracias chivito.

Kathy Melanese would like to thank her parents for their unwavering belief in her ability to accomplish anything she desired; Trevor, Amanda, and Nicholas, who are the light of her life and make her smile every day; her husband, who makes her dreams come true; the amazingly dedicated teachers and students of National City; and finally, her coauthors, who provided an incredible experience in learning and collaboration.

Teaching Math to English Language Learners 1

If you are a classroom teacher, it is likely that you have students in your class for whom English is a second language. It is also likely that, while language arts is their biggest challenge of the school day, these students are struggling in mathematics. Achievement data show that English language learners (ELLs) are not performing at the same levels as their native English-speaking counterparts (NAEP 2007). This inequity can be addressed if teachers provide well-designed extra support for their students.

Why should teachers have to address English language development (ELD) during the precious academic time allotted to the instruction of mathematics? After all, in many schools across the United States, ELD has its own mandated daily instructional minutes. And teachers have learned strategies for helping English language learners understand their lessons. Isn't the incorporation of visuals, the use of manipulatives, and a conscious effort to read word problems aloud enough to address the needs of these students?

English language learners need to learn the content of their mathematics courses. But learning is mediated through language—in our case, the English language. Every part of learning is language dependent, from the arousal of a curiosity, to the teacher's explanation of a concept, to the formation of an understanding of that concept, to the verbalization or written expression of that understanding. Along the path from curiosity to demonstrated understanding, a learner—any learner—needs to clarify his developing understanding, test hypotheses, and solicit confirmation of his thinking. All of these activities are conducted through the medium of language. When a learner is carrying out all of this cognitive work in a second language, limitations in language can lead to limitations in learning. Compounding this situation is the time crunch that faces students of mathematics: each year math becomes more challenging and more abstract. Therefore, in classrooms where instruction is provided only in English, the more support provided to English language learners, the sooner they can enter and appreciate the world of mathematics.

This book is intended to assist teachers in helping their students accomplish two goals: develop their proficiency in English and develop their mathematical understanding. To that end, the lessons in the book seek to amplify rather than simplify the role of language in math class. The lessons show different ways that teachers can explicitly structure experiences so that all students, especially ELLs, can engage in conversations about math in English that promote better understanding of the content being taught.

To accomplish these goals, it is important for teachers to be aware of the factors that contribute to English language learners' success in mathematics. These include the backgrounds and experiences that these students bring to the classroom; how students acquire a second language; the challenges ELLs face when learning mathematics; determining the linguistic demands of a math lesson; and specific strategies and activities that simultaneously support learning English and learning mathematics with understanding.

The Backgrounds of English Language Learners

There are approximately five million ELLs enrolled in public schools in the United States (National Clearinghouse for English Language Acquisition 2007). That's more than 10 percent of the school population. And every year, the percentage of ELLs increases. In some states, ELLs represent a far larger portion of the school population. In California, for example, more than 25 percent of students are English language learners (California Department of Education 2006–2007). Texas, New York, Florida, Illinois, and Arizona also have substantial numbers of students who are learning English as a second language.

In some states, the school population of English language learners is relatively not as large, but the percent increase in recent years is significant. In the southeastern United States, for example, the ELL population in schools has increased more than 200 percent in the last ten years (National Clearinghouse for English Language Acquisition 2007).

The profiles of English language learners vary in the length of time they've been in the United States and in the amount of schooling they received in their home country. The educational backgrounds of ELLs range from recent arrivals with little or no schooling, or interrupted schooling in their country of origin, to those who have a high degree of literacy in their native language. And there are those students whose families have been in the United States for one or two generations and have maintained their native language at home but have not yet acquired enough English to be proficient in academic settings.

ELLs are enrolled in different types of programs in school, depending on the resources and philosophies of the state or district they are educated in. Many states offer bilingual education in a student's primary language as well as English. This allows students to continue their conceptual growth and literacy skills in the primary language while adding English. When children are provided an education in their first language, they get two things: academic knowledge and literacy skills. Both the knowledge and the literacy skills students develop in their first language help English language development enormously. The knowledge students acquire using their first language makes the input they hear and read in English much more comprehensible. This results in more language acquisition and more learning in general (Krashen and Terrell 1983). TESOL (Teachers of English to Speakers of Other Languages) sees the maintenance and promotion of students' native languages as an important part of effective education for students learning English (TESOL 2006).

In locations where bilingual education is unavailable because of different factors (no teachers speak the students' language, district or state policies, parent input), ELLs are placed in English-only classrooms, and in some schools and districts they receive English language development as part of the day. Some districts offer newcomer programs for recent immigrants to help them learn some basic survival English and become acquainted with American culture.

The length of time English language learners have been in the United States, the amount of schooling they have had in their home country, and the kinds of support they have received here in our schools all affect their progress in acquiring English. As well, any instruction, including math, that is delivered in English affects students' English language development.

English Language Development

Considering the importance that acquiring English has on learning in the content areas, English language development instruction should be based on sound theoretical principles of how children acquire a second language. Dutro and Moran (2003) discuss the differences between the theories of the natural acquisition of English (Krashen and Terrell 1983), which is the idea that language can be acquired in a natural way through meaningful interactions, similar to how we acquire our first language, and the direct instruction of English (McLaughlin 1985). Dutro and Moran argue that there needs to be a balance between the two theories, stating that "a comprehensive theory of classroom instruction should incorporate both informal and formal-language learning opportunities" (228).

Fillmore and Snow (2000) echo this idea by explaining that certain conditions must be present for children to be successful in learning English. They state that ELLs must interact directly and frequently with people who are expert speakers of English, which mirrors the natural process of language acquisition; however, if that condition is not met for any reason, then direct instruction in English is essential for language learning. Regardless of ELLs' primary language or school experience, we can maximize their academic opportunities by providing direct instruction for learning English that is embedded in a natural, meaningful context with many opportunities for practice. The lessons in this book were developed to include both informal and formal language learning opportunities in math class.

Another aspect of instruction for ELLs is that teachers need to use strategies that give students access to the content in mathematics and other curriculum areas, and help them learn the sophisticated vocabulary and language structures required in those academic settings. This focus on English as a language, not just as a means of instruction, should cut across all content areas and should be at the forefront of teachers' thinking when planning a lesson. In other words, when we teach math to English language learners, we are also teaching English, not just teaching *in* English. Dutro and Moran (2003) have called this teaching of language prior to content instruction *frontloading*. Dutro, in conjunction with the California Reading and Literature Project, has developed frontloading approaches for language arts curricula in California. We offer here an approach to frontloading English academic language in math.

The Challenges of Teaching Math to English Language Learners

Many educators share the misconception that because it uses symbols, mathematics is not associated with any language or culture and is ideal for facilitating the transition of recent immigrant students into

English instruction (Garrison 1997). To the contrary, language plays an important role in learning mathematics. Teachers use language to explain mathematical concepts and carry out math procedures. While solving problems in mathematics, we often use specialized technical vocabulary (*addition, subtraction, addend, sum*). And researchers of mathematical learning have found that students can deepen their understanding of mathematics by using language to communicate and reflect on their ideas and cement their understandings. Classroom talk can cause misconceptions to surface, helping teachers recognize what students do and do not understand. When students talk about their mathematical thinking, it can help them improve their ability to reason logically (Chapin and Johnson 2006, Cobb et al. 1997, Hiebert and Wearne 1993, Khisty 1995, Lampert 1990, Wood 1999).

The challenge of teaching math to English language learners lies not only in making math lessons comprehensible to students but also in ensuring that students have the language needed to understand instruction and express their grasp of math concepts both orally and with written language. ELLs have the dual task of learning a second language and content simultaneously. For this reason, "it is critical to set both content and language objectives for ELLs. Just as language cannot occur if we only focus on subject matter, content knowledge cannot grow if we only focus on learning the English language" (Hill and Flynn 2006, 22).

English language learners are faced with some common obstacles when learning math. One challenge they face is unknown or misunderstood vocabulary. For example, they can become confused during a discussion if the mathematics vocabulary has different meanings in everyday usage, as with *even, odd*, and *function*. They also may be confused if the same mathematical operation can be signaled with a variety of mathematics terms, such as *add, and, plus, sum*, and *combine*. A word such as *left*—as in "How many are *left*?"—can be confusing when the directional meaning of the word is most commonly used in everyday English. The words *sum* and *whole* also can cause confusion because they have nonmathematical homonyms (*some* and *hole*).

A second obstacle is with an incomplete understanding of syntax and grammar. For example, math questions are often embedded in language that makes the problems unclear or difficult to comprehend. Consider the following problem:

Samuel bought three bags of oranges with seven oranges in each bag. How many oranges did he buy?

This word problem uses both the past and present tense of the irregular verb *to buy* in one question, which may cause difficulty for an English language learner, depending on the student's English language proficiency.

Consider another problem:

Lisa gave a total of 12 treats to her cats.
She gave her large cat 2 more treats than she gave her small cat.
How many treats did she give to each cat?

Here, students need to understand or figure out the meanings of words such as *total* and *treats*. They also need to understand words that convey a mathematical relationship such as *more . . . than*. In addition, students need to infer that Lisa has only two cats.

English language learners typically experience difficulty understanding and therefore solving word problems, and this difficulty increases in the later grades of elementary school as the word problems become more linguistically and conceptually complex. Difficulty with grammar, syntax, and vocabulary lies in both understanding math instruction and having the ability to engage in discussions about math.

Many teachers use strategies to help students understand the content in their math lessons. Scaffolds for learning may include manipulatives, visuals, and graphics. These supports are all essential for building a cursory understanding of math concepts, but they may not provide students enough linguistic support for them to discuss their thinking, which would lead to a deeper understanding of content. For example, let's say that a student's understanding of polygons is based on a two-column chart with drawings that distinguish polygons from shapes that are not polygons. Once the chart is put away, the student may not have internalized enough of the linguistic elements of the lesson to be able to continue her learning in subsequent lessons on polygons. Having the language to talk about math concepts is crucial to developing an understanding of those concepts.

Classroom discussions about math have been shown to deepen students' conceptual understanding. These discussions are a critical aspect of the development of language and content, providing a setting for English language learners to negotiate meaning in daily instructional interactions (García 2003). However, if the language needed to engage in these discussions is not made explicit, ELLs are less likely to benefit from mathematical discussions and can fall further behind their peers.

The challenge for teachers is to focus on math concepts *and* the academic language that is specific to mathematics. Teachers must be cognizant of the linguistic demands of their lessons and how they will address those demands explicitly during instruction so that ELLs can fully participate.

Determining the Linguistic Demands of a Math Lesson

Before providing specific support for ELLs in mathematics, we first need to consider the linguistic demands of a math lesson. This involves determining what academic language students will need to understand and use and knowing how much of the English language students are capable of understanding and producing.

Social or conversational language is the language that students use in familiar, face-to-face situations. This is different than academic language, which includes knowledge of technical and less frequently used vocabulary and ways of speaking English that are not usually heard or used in everyday conversation. The academic language of mathematics includes specialized vocabulary (*polygon*, *sides*, *vertices*, *corners*, *open*, *closed*, *straight*, *curved*) and the language structures and grammar needed to use the vocabulary ("*The* shape *is not a* polygon *because it has* curved sides *and it is* open.").

The publishers of math textbooks often make note of the academic vocabulary being introduced in a particular lesson. Frequently, however, there is no direction provided, either to the teacher or to the students, on how to correctly use the new terms. Just because an English learner is told the meaning of a new word does not mean he can construct a coherent sentence (thought) using that term. Simply knowing the term does not allow the learner to use it to express or develop understanding or learning related to the concept. For example, an English learner might be taught the term *polygon*, but that does not mean that same student can draw conclusions, either orally or in writing, about a particular shape and determine whether or not it is a polygon. And if the English learner cannot construct the sentences necessary to talk about particular figures, how does the teacher know what the student has learned?

Once teachers have identified what academic language students will need to know and understand in a particular math lesson, they can then plan strategies for supporting students' ability to use the language in order to carry on mathematical discussions in English. To provide the appropriate support, teachers must be aware that there are varying levels of proficiency with language acquisition.

Given that many teachers have a wide range of levels in their class, from beginning ELLs to fully proficient native English speakers, it can be overwhelming to figure out how to meet all of their needs in one math lesson. It is important, however, for classroom teachers to know each student's level of English proficiency. The descriptions of the levels of English language proficiency differ from state to state. In California, for example, the California English Language Development Test (CELDT) identifies the levels as beginning, early intermediate, intermediate, early advanced, and advanced. In the state of Washington, the levels of English language proficiency are beginning, advanced beginning, intermediate, advanced, and transitional. In Illinois, the levels are described as follows: beginning, developing, expanding, and bridging.

In this book, we identify the English language proficiency levels as beginning, intermediate, and advanced. What's important is that teachers recognize that there *are* different levels of English language proficiency, and that the kind of support they give to students often depends upon how much of the second language students are capable of understanding and producing.

Specific Strategies and Activities That Simultaneously Support Learning English and Learning Math

There are a variety of effective strategies and activities that teachers can use in a lesson that will help all students, particularly English language learners, understand math content and develop English language skills. The use of gestures, manipulatives, charts, and graphs, for example, helps students understand the math content when it is being taught in English. Other strategies and activities, such as the use of sentence frames (e.g., *This is a* _____. *It is/has* _____.) and allowing time for class discussions, provide students with the support and the opportunity to talk about their mathematical ideas in English and actively use the language of mathematics.

While the use of the following strategies and activities in a math lesson can benefit all students, it is essential for ELLs.

Activate prior knowledge.

Prior knowledge provides the foundation for interpreting new information, and it enables all students, especially English language learners, to make inferences about the meaning of words and expressions that they may not have come across before. The more connections we can make to students' experiences and interests, the more relevance math is likely to assume in students' minds and lives.

Reduce the stress level in the room.

Create a low-stress environment that encourages expression of ideas; where mathematical mistakes are seen as opportunities for learning; and where linguistic mistakes such as incorrect grammar do not inhibit the recognition of good mathematical thinking.

Use sentence frames.

Sentence frames serve a variety of purposes. They provide the support English language learners need in order to fully participate in math discussions; they serve to contextualize and bring meaning to vocabulary; they provide a structure for practicing and extending English language skills; and they help students use the vocabulary they learn in grammatically correct and complete sentences. When appropriate, sentence frames also provide the scaffolding young learners need in order to express their comprehension of math ideas in writing.

Create vocabulary banks.

Charts that contain key math vocabulary and phrases are helpful references for ELLs when discussing or writing about their math thinking, especially if the words are accompanied with illustrations.

Practice wait time.

After asking a question, wait for a while before calling on a volunteer. This gives all students, especially English language learners, time to process questions and formulate responses.

Use native language as a resource.

Teachers who know the native language of their students can preview and review vocabulary in the native language. Teachers can also ask students to help others in the class by having them translate, define, and clarify English terms in the students' native language.

In addition, if the students' native language shares cognates with English, these cognates can be pointed out and used to help students understand terms. Cognates are words that share the same ancestral origins and therefore are very similar in two different languages (e.g., *difference* and *diferencia* are English and Spanish cognates). For cognates to be useful, students must know the meaning of the words in their primary language. Lists of cognates are available from a variety of sources. We recommend starting with *The ESL Teacher's Book of Lists*

(Kress 1993). The FOSS science series (1993) and the *CORE Reading Resource* (Honig, Diamond, and Gutlohn 2007) are also good resources.

Make manipulative materials available.

Manipulatives serve a variety of purposes and are important tools that can make math content comprehensible to English language learners. Manipulatives give students ways to construct physical models of abstract mathematical ideas; they build students' confidence by giving them a way to test and confirm their reasoning; they are useful tools for solving problems; and they make learning math interesting and enjoyable. Manipulatives can also facilitate effective communication by providing a referent for talking about mathematical ideas (Hiebert et al. 1997).

Ask questions that elicit explanations.

Asking good questions can prompt English language learners to discuss their thinking and elaborate on their ideas. Ask questions that elicit more than a yes or no response, such as

- ✦ What do you think the answer will be? Why do you think that?
- ✦ What is this problem about?
- ✦ What's the first thing you'll do to solve the problem?

Design questions for different proficiency levels.

Questioning students lets teachers know what students have learned. Answering questions lets students test, confirm, or modify their own understandings. None of these goals can be met unless the questions are structured in a way that produces a response from the students.

Following are examples of questions for students with different proficiency levels in English.

Beginning Level
English language learners are not always able to answer the questions posed to them, especially when questions are open-ended. A teacher can provide support and improve participation of students with lower levels of English proficiency by using a prompt that requires a physical response:

- ✦ Show me the circle.
- ✦ Touch the larger number.

Teachers can also ask a question with a yes or no answer:

+ Is one number larger than the other?

When asking short-answer questions, the teacher can build the answer into the question for additional support:

+ Is this a triangle or a circle?
+ Is the line horizontal or vertical?
+ Should we add or subtract?

Intermediate and Advanced Levels
Students with intermediate and advanced levels of proficiency need less support to understand and respond to questions from the teacher, but carefully crafted questions can improve the quality of both their responses and their English. For example, instead of asking an intermediate or advanced student, "How did you solve the problem?" you might phrase your question this way: "What did you do first, second, and third to solve the problem?" The second question models the structure of a well-crafted answer: "First, I put the blocks in groups of ten. Second, I counted by tens. Third, I added the ones left over." Compare that with the response more likely from the first question: "I counted them."

Use prompts to support student responses.

Prompts can help English language learners get started when responding to a question:

+ You figured it out by . . .
+ It is a polygon because . . .
+ First you put the hexagon on the table, and then . . .

Provide visuals.

Visuals enable students to see a basic concept much more effectively than if we rely only on words. Among the visuals we can use in presenting math content are pictures and photographs, real objects, graphic organizers, drawings on the overhead projector, and charts.

Pose problems in familiar contexts.

When a problem is embedded in a familiar context, English language learners have an easier time understanding the problem's structure and discussing how to solve it.

Elicit nonverbal responses (e.g., thumbs up or down).

Nonverbal responses help teachers check for understanding without requiring students to produce language. English language learners can participate and show that they understand a concept, or agree or disagree with someone's idea, without having to talk. This is especially important for students whose comprehension of English is more advanced than their ability to speak the language.

Demonstrate and model.

When teachers model their thinking or demonstrate an example of how to do an activity in a clear and explicit manner, it helps ELLs get a picture of what to do.

Use dramatization and gestures.

Supplementing verbal discussion with gestures, pantomime, or dramatization can help English language learners bring meaning to explanations, directions, vocabulary, and word problems.

Modify teacher talk.

Speak slowly and use clear articulation. Reduce the amount of teacher talk and use a variety of words for the same idea. Exaggerate intonation and place more stress on important new concepts or questions.

Recast mathematical ideas and terms.

Mathematics has many linguistic features that can be problematic for English language learners. Use synonyms for mathematical words, such as *subtract*, *take away*, and *minus*. At the same time, be aware that using too many terms simultaneously can confuse ELLs.

Consider language *and* math skills when grouping students.

There are times when grouping students with like abilities in math makes sense, especially when those students are all struggling with the same concept or skill. Most of the time, however, students benefit from working in groups where students have varying skill levels in mathematics.

Students also benefit from working in groups where students have different levels of English language competence. However, it is important for teachers to monitor student talk to ensure that all students have the opportunity to engage in mathematical conversations.

Facilitate whole-class discussions.

In a whole-class discussion, the teacher is not engaged in delivering information or quizzing. Rather, she is attempting to give students the chance to engage in sustained reasoning. The teacher facilitates and guides, and the focus is on students' thinking (Chapin, O'Connor, and Anderson 2003).

Allow for small-group discussions.

In a small-group discussion, the teacher typically gives students a question to talk about among themselves, in groups of three to six. The teacher circulates, listening in on discussions, asking questions, and assisting when necessary.

Utilize partner talk.

In partner talk, the teacher asks a question and then gives students a minute or two to put their thoughts into words with their nearest neighbor. Partner talk allows more students to participate in classroom discussions.

Ask for choral responses from students.

When teachers have students echo back a word or phrase, it exposes students to new vocabulary and serves as a model for correct pronunciation, syntax, and grammar.

Rephrase strategies and ideas.

Rephrasing is when the teacher or a student explains a strategy or an idea, in English, that someone else in the group has shared. Rephrasing gives English language learners another opportunity to make sense of an idea. When students rephrase another student's idea or strategy, it helps clarify their thinking and cement their understanding.

Connect symbols with words.

When strategies for solving problems are described, write the number sentences and point to the symbols (such as $+$, $\times$, and $=$), stressing the words in English.

Putting It All Together: How This Book Is Organized

The lessons in *Supporting English Language Learners in Math Class* are designed to help students understand math content and develop their English language skills. While the lessons span the math curriculum, the book isn't intended to provide all the needed lessons for English language learners. Rather, the lessons are meant to serve as examples of how best to provide the necessary support these students require.

Topics for lessons in the book include geometry, arithmetic word problems, data analysis, algebra, and number sense. The lessons were taught to students from a variety of ethnic and socioeconomic backgrounds, whose native languages include English, Spanish, Vietnamese, Chinese, Cambodian, Farsi, Arabic, Tagalog, Russian, Somali, and Punjabi.

Each math lesson is preceded by a minilesson that explicitly introduces and teaches the academic language that students will need to understand and use during the actual math lesson. In the minilesson, sentence frames are introduced. The sentence frames are crucial and serve a variety of purposes. Sentence frames provide the support ELLs need in order to fully participate in math discussions; they serve to contextualize and bring meaning to the vocabulary; they provide a structure for practicing and extending English language skills; they help students use the vocabulary they learn in grammatically correct and complete sentences; and they allow for differentiated instruction because they are designed for different levels of English language proficiency. For example, the following frames support students at various language levels in their discussions about polygons:

Beginning

A _____ has _____.

It has _____.

Intermediate and Advanced

A _____ has _____, _____, and _____.

My shape has _____, _____, and _____.

I built my shape with a _____ and a _____.

It looks like a _____.

Following the minilesson, the actual math lesson begins. Now, the English language learners in the class have the support they need to fully participate in class discussions, using language to develop their understanding of math content.

Throughout the lessons, students practice using different language functions, depending on the mathematics that is being taught and the sentence frames used. For example, the following sentence frame helps students describe nouns, such as polygons:

This is a _____. It is/has _____.

This sentence frame helps students to compare and contrast:

A _____ has _____, but a _____ has _____.

Other frames assist students in describing a sequence of events:

First, _____.

Next, _____.

Then, _____.

After that, _____.

Finally, _____.

Other frames help students make predictions:

I predict that _____ because _____.

The lessons in this book help students learn to use a variety of language functions while discussing their mathematical ideas in English.

These functions include describing nouns, explaining cause and effect, comparing and contrasting, sequencing, describing location, hypothesizing, categorizing, predicting, giving and following directions, making inferences, drawing conclusions, and summarizing.

Each lesson in the book contains the following:

+ grade-level recommendations
+ an overview that gives a concise summary of the lesson: what students will be doing and learning
+ a math goal and a language goal
+ key vocabulary words
+ a materials list
+ a variety of sentence frames for different language levels to support language production
+ a class profile that provides information regarding the English language proficiency levels of the students in the vignette
+ a vignette from the classroom has two parts: one introduces academic language and sentence frames to support language production, and the other focuses on the actual math lesson; during each vignette, specific strategies for supporting English language learners are described
+ student work samples
+ step-by-step directions for the lesson

In addition to the sample lessons, we've included a chapter titled "Helping English Language Learners Make Sense of Math Word Problems." Because word problems can be so difficult for English learners to read and understand, and therefore solve, we've provided detailed examples of strategies that teachers can use to help English learners navigate word problems while developing their English language skills.

We've also included a chapter on how to modify math lessons to support English learners. Here, we describe our thinking and planning behind each lesson: how we identified the language demands and developed the sentence frames, and why we chose particular instructional strategies.

And finally, in Chapter 10, "Frequently Asked Questions," we address teachers' concerns and key questions about supporting English language learners in math class.

Meeting the Challenge

Mathematics is the gatekeeper to higher education. In fact, the more mathematics that students take in middle school and high school, the more likely they are to go on to college (U.S. Department of Education 2000). Because English language learners are not achieving at the same levels in math as their native English-speaking counterparts, many are at risk of having the gate to higher education closed to them. Fortunately, teachers *can* make a difference and address this inequity by providing well-designed support so that English learners can develop proficiency in English *and* develop their mathematical understanding.

The prospect of leveling the playing field so that all students have equal access to the math content being taught is exciting yet challenging. Meeting this challenge will require extra support, the kind of assistance that this book describes. It is our hope that teachers view the lessons in *Supporting English Language Learners in Math Class* as models and apply the strategies to their own experiences as they help *all* of their students succeed in mathematics.

2 Capture and Double Capture

An Arithmetic Lesson

Day 1: Grades K, 1, and 2
Day 2: Grades 1 and 2

Overview

In this lesson, children use playing cards to play the games *Capture* and *Double Capture*. The games give students experience with counting, comparing numbers, using the concepts of greater than and less than, and adding quantities. Repeated opportunities to play the games help children develop fluency with arithmetic thinking as they encounter the same numbers again and again.

In a minilesson prior to playing the games, sentence frames and key vocabulary are introduced to help all students, especially English language learners, compare numbers and sums and explain their strategies for figuring sums.

Math Goal: Compare numbers and sums; develop and use strategies for computation

Language Goal: Compare numbers and sums; explain strategies for combining numbers

Key Vocabulary: add/plus, count(ed), double(s), equal, greater than, subtract/take away, sum

Materials

✦ 5 sentence strips or pieces of construction paper for sentence frames

✦ decks of playing cards (with face cards removed), 1 per pair of students

✦ optional: 1 deck of jumbo playing cards for modeling the lesson

Sentence Frames That Help Students Compare Numbers and Compare Sums

I have _____. You have _____.

_____ is greater than _____.

_____ is equal to _____.

Sentence Frames That Help Students Explain Their Strategies for Combining Numbers

First _____, then _____.

I know that _____, so _____.

Class Profile

Of the twenty students in Frannie McKenzie's class, two are beginning English language learners (ELLs), six are English language learners with intermediate fluency, three are advanced English learners, and nine are native English speakers.

From the Classroom ✦ **Day 1: Capture**

Minilesson Introducing Academic Language

Christine Sphar greeted the students in Frannie McKenzie's class as they gathered on the perimeter of the rug at the front of the room.

"Today we're going to play a card game," Christine told the class. The children's faces lit up upon hearing the word *game*. Playing games is a great way to provide practice with skills and concepts that have already been introduced in whole-class lessons. Games provide a motivating reason for practice and an interesting context for discussing ideas that can further students' understanding of math *and* develop their English language skills.

To tap their prior experience, Christine asked the students to turn to a partner and share what they knew about playing cards. When conversations died down, Christine counted down from five to regain the students' attention and asked them what kinds of information they had shared with each other.

"You can play games with them," Adrianna offered. "We just learned how to play *Tens Go Fish* in our class."

"Cards have numbers on them," Jade shared.

Sebastian, an intermediate-level English learner, exclaimed, "And they have pictures of queens and kings!"

"They also have jacks!" Ricardo chimed in. "And they come in red and black and have different signs on them."

"Sounds like you all know a lot about playing cards," Christine commented.

From a jumbo-size deck of playing cards, Christine pulled out the face cards and held a few of them up for the students to see. She explained, "Today we're going to play a game with the playing cards. For the game, we won't need the face cards; those are the kings, queens, and jacks. We only need the aces, which stand for one, and the cards two through ten."

"The first game we're going to play is called *Capture*," Christine told the class. To make sure everyone knew what the word meant, she asked for an explanation.

"Capture is like when you catch a wild animal," McKenna explained.

"Yeah, it's when you get something and keep it," Dasia added.

"That's right. When you *capture* something, you get it and keep it," Christine said, exaggerating her tone when saying the word *capture* and using her hands to illustrate grabbing and keeping something. Supplementing verbal discussion with gestures, pantomime, or dramatization can help English language learners bring meaning to explanations, directions, and vocabulary.

As she modeled, Christine directed the students to pantomime capturing something and say the word aloud together. When they were finished, Christine said, "Today, we're going to *capture* cards. I'll show you how the game works."

Using the jumbo-size cards, Christine modeled an easy way to shuffle the cards by placing them facedown and swirling them around with her hands. This mixes the cards well and is much easier for small hands than traditional shuffling. Using Sebastian as her partner, Christine showed the class how to deal the cards so that each player had an equal number.

"Before you start playing, each player has to have a stack of cards facedown in front of him," Christine said, pointing to her stack of cards, then to Sebastian's. "I'm going to pretend that I'm playing with Sebastian. Each of us turns over the top card from our own pile." Christine and Sebastian both did this; Christine turned over a 9 and Sebastian turned over a 2.

Christine then introduced the following sentence frames and told the students that the frames would help her and Sebastian compare their numbers. She had the students say the sentence frames aloud in a choral voice, pausing for the blank spaces. For younger children who are not yet reading, the sentence frames are used orally; the teacher models and the students repeat the frame.

I have _____. You have _____.

_____ is greater than _____.

When they were finished, Christine modeled using the frames. "Since my card was greater," she began, "I have to say, 'I have nine. You have two. Nine is greater than two.'"

When she was finished, Christine had the class repeat what she had said. Then she wrote the words *greater than* on the class vocabulary chart.

"Who knows other words that mean the same as *greater than*?" she asked.

"More than!"

"Bigger than!"

Recasting mathematical ideas and terms can help ELLs understand the meaning of new vocabulary words. However, Christine is careful not to confuse students by introducing too many words simultaneously.

Christine continued playing *Capture* with Sebastian, eliciting ideas from the class. Each time they put their cards down on the rug, Christine

Capture and Double Capture

asked the students to tell which number was greater. She then had the class use the sentence frames to practice comparing the two numbers.

Christine reminded the students that when they played with a partner, the player with the greater number could not take the cards until he or she compared the quantities using the sentence frames. This rule would motivate and encourage the students to use language to compare quantities.

As they were modeling the game for the class, Sebastian and Christine each placed a 7 on the carpet on one of their turns.

"What happens now?" Christine asked the class.

"They're the same number!" several students called out.

"What math word can we use?" Christine asked.

When no one responded, Christine prompted, "Seven and seven are . . ."

"Equal!" Lila exclaimed.

Christine wrote the word *equal* on the vocabulary chart, writing the equals sign next to the word to connect the word with a symbol. She then introduced the following sentence frame and had the students practice, pausing for the blank spaces.

_____ *is equal to* _____.

"Seven is equal to seven!" the students chorused along with Christine.

"We can also say that seven is the same as seven," Christine added.

"When you and your partner's cards are equal, each player takes back her own card," Christine explained. Sebastian and Christine modeled this for the class.

Christine continued playing *Capture* with Sebastian and the class until the game was over and all the cards had been played. Together with the class, Sebastian counted his cards and then Christine's cards to see who had more.

Playing the Game

After modeling the game of *Capture*, Christine reviewed how to shuffle the cards and deal them, then dismissed the students to their seats and gave each pair a deck of cards. As they played, Christine walked around the room, checking in with partners to see if they understood the directions and to make sure that they were using language to compare the quantities on the cards. She paid particular attention to Ahmed and Rinor, the two beginning English learners, making sure that these students knew how to use the sentence frames for support.

Many of the students were able to correctly use the sentence frames as they compared the quantities on the cards. Some students experimented with language that they were most comfortable using. Christine listened in on a game between Sean, a student with intermediate fluency, and Ahmed, a beginning English learner.

"I have nine and he has one," Sean said. "I got the most so I get the cards."

Next, Sean put down a 2 and Ahmed put down an 8.

"He have two; I have eight," Ahmed said. "I get to pick these; eight is more than two." Ahmed took the two cards, and then the boys each placed more cards on the table: Sean put down a 5 and Ahmed, a 2.

"I got the greater; he got the lower," Sean said. "I win."

"So five is greater than two," Christine said, modeling correct grammar. Christine was pleased that Sean was beginning to use mathematical language to compare the quantities. She continued listening in on their game for a few more seconds and encouraged them to use the sentence frames for support.

When partners had the chance to play at least two games of *Capture*, Christine had them put their cards away and brought an end to math time.

✦ Day 2: Double Capture

The next day, Christine called the students to the rug to model a new version of the game of *Capture*. To begin, she took the jumbo-size cards and shuffled them. Kelly volunteered to deal them out, one by one. When all the cards had been dealt, Christine introduced *Double Capture*. She wrote the word *double* on the vocabulary chart and asked the class what the word meant.

"It's like twins!" José said.

Max, a native English speaker, explained, "It means two numbers that are the same, like five and five."

"I know my doubles!" McKenna exclaimed. "Two plus two is four!"

"Double one is two and double two is four," Alyssa offered.

"There are a couple of ways to think about the word *double*," Christine acknowledged. "*Double* can mean a number that is twice as much as another number, like Alyssa said, or two numbers that are the same or identical like twins, as José mentioned."

Christine then continued to explain the rules for the new game. "In *Double Capture*, you each turn over two cards at once instead of one card; that's why the game is called *Double Capture*. Then you *add* the numbers together." Christine wrote the word *add* on the vocabulary chart and drew the addition symbol next to it to make a connection between the word and the sign for the students. She also wrote the word *plus* next to *add*, providing a synonym that might be more familiar to the class.

To show an example, Christine put two cards down on the carpet in front of her: a 2 and a 7. She then said, "Each player adds the numbers together, and the player with the greater *sum* wins the round and gets to keep all four cards."

As she said the word *sum*, Christine wrote it on the vocabulary chart. "*Sum* is the answer to an addition problem," she told the class. "Two plus two equals . . ."

"Four!" the students shot back.

"So four is the *sum*, or answer, to two plus two," Christine clarified. She had the students practice the word *sum* by saying it aloud several times. She then wrote these two sentences on the board, reading them aloud with the class:

> *The <u>sum</u> of two plus two is four.*

> *I want <u>some</u> cookies.*

"*Sum* and *some* sound the same, but they are spelled differently and have different meanings," Christine pointed out.

Some math words have nonmathematical homonyms that can cause confusion for English learners. Bringing these features of language to the forefront in math class benefits all students, especially English language learners.

Next, Kelly put down two cards in front of her: a 4 and a 3. Using the sentence frames introduced the previous day during the game of *Capture*, Christine and Kelly compared their sums; Christine went first to model.

"I have nine and you have seven. Nine is greater than seven." When she was finished, Christine directed the students to repeat what she'd said, giving them an opportunity to practice. She also reminded the students that in *Double Capture*, the partner with the greater sum had to compare the sums using the sentence frames *before* he could take the cards.

Christine then asked Kelly, "How did you know that the sum, or answer, was seven?"

Kelly, an intermediate-level English speaker, needed some help explaining her strategy.

"What did you do first?" Christine inquired.

"I counted," Kelly said.

"What number did you start with?" Christine asked, pointing to Kelly's playing cards:

"I started with the four," Kelly replied.

"And then what did you do?" Christine asked, continuing to probe Kelly's thinking.

"I counted three more," Kelly explained.

"So first you started with four, then you counted on three more," Christine summarized. "When you explain how you combine the numbers on the two cards, you can use sentence frames to help you."

Christine introduced the following frame and had the class read it aloud, pausing for the blank spaces:

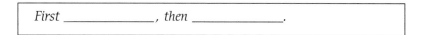

First _____, *then* _____.

She then modeled Kelly's strategy, using the sentence frame. "First I started with four, then I counted on three more." Christine had the students practice by having them echo back what she had said.

"My sum was greater, so I get to keep all four cards," Christine noted, reminding the class how a player wins a round.

To make sure students understood how to play, Christine and Kelly each placed two more cards in front of them on the rug. Christine put down a 7 and a 4; Kelly placed a 6 and a 5. Christine added her numbers first, thinking aloud to model a strategy for the students.

"I know that seven and three is ten," Christine explained, pointing to the 7 of clubs and three of the four hearts. "I'm always looking for ways to make a ten when I'm adding numbers together."

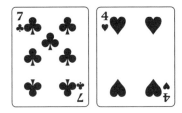

She continued, "So then I added one more heart and got eleven."

Christine then introduced another sentence frame that would also help students explain their strategies. She had the class read the frame, pausing for the blank spaces.

I know that _____ , so _____ .

Christine repeated her strategy, using the sentence frame, and then had the class echo back to her as she pointed to the symbols on her cards. "I know that seven and three is ten, so I added one more heart and got eleven."

Kelly went next, pointing first to the 6, and then to each of the five clubs on the 5 card. She counted, "Six, seven, eight, nine, ten, eleven."

To help Kelly explain her strategy with words, Christine pointed to the sentence frame on the board:

First _____ , then _____ .

With Christine's assistance, Kelly said, "First I started with the six, then I counted five more and got eleven."

"Both answers are the same!" Jade exclaimed.

"That's correct," Christine confirmed. She pointed to one of the sentence frames from the day before and said, "Eleven is equal to eleven." The class echoed back.

"When both sums are *equal*, or the *same amount*, each player just takes back her own cards and then puts two new cards down to play another round," Christine explained.

In modeling the game, Christine had purposely provided the students with two sentence frames that would help them explain several strategies for combining numbers. She had created these frames because she knew they would fit for the following strategies that children commonly use when combining numbers:

Solving for 6 + 5

Strategy	Example	Sentence Frame
Counting from 1	1, 2, 3, 4, 5, 6, 7, 8, 9, 10, 11 or 1, 2, 3, 4, 5, 6, 7, 8, 9, 10, 11	*First* _____, *then* _____.
Counting on from 6	6, 7, 8, 9, 10, 11	*First* _____, *then* _____.
Counting on from 5	5, 6, 7, 8, 9, 10, 11	*First* _____, *then* _____.
Making a 10 (or doubles plus 1)	5 + 5 is 10, and 1 more is 11	*I know that* _____, *so* _____.
Doubles minus 1	6 + 6 is 12, minus 1 is 11	*I know that* _____, *so* _____.

Christine is careful to encourage students to try to explain their strategies first on their own. If students need help, they can find support from one frame or the other depending on the strategy used. The frames are there to support language production, not to dictate which strategy students should use or limit their use of language.

In addition to the sentence frames, Christine had introduced some key vocabulary words that students could use to compare sums and to explain their strategies: *greater than, equal, add* and *plus, sum,* and *double(s)*. Christine also included the words *subtract* and *take away* on the vocabulary list in case students used strategies involving subtraction (e.g., doubles minus one).

When she was finished modeling *Double Capture*, Christine handed out decks of cards to pairs of students and dismissed them to their seats, and play ensued.

As they played, Christine circulated and observed the students, keeping the following questions in mind:

✦ Do the students understand the rules of *Double Capture*?
✦ What strategies are they using when combining two numbers?

◆ Are students' strategies accurate and efficient?

◆ Are students using language to compare sums?

A Class Discussion

After students had time to play two games of *Double Capture*, Christine directed them to put their cards away and then called them to the rug for a class discussion.

To begin, Christine asked the students if they got a really big sum while playing the games. This question was designed to assess students' number sense: did they have an idea of what a big sum was in the game?

Christine listened as students reported a variety of sums, ranging from thirteen to twenty. When they were finished, Christine commented, "Those are all big sums to get in the game! But how did you figure out those sums? How did you figure the answers when you added two cards together?" She then held up two jumbo-size cards and asked the students to find the sum of nine and four.

After providing some think time, Christine directed the class to whisper the answer aloud. She then called on Owen, who volunteered to come up to the front of the class and explain how he solved the problem.

Using one of the sentence frames for support, Owen said, "I know that nine and one is ten, so ten and three is thirteen." As he explained, Owen first touched the 9 of diamonds, and then pointed to one of the spades on the 4 of spades to make ten. Finally, he counted the three remaining spades to get to thirteen.

"So Owen made a ten and then counted the rest of the spades on this card," Christine summarized, pointing to the cards.

Next, Christine held up two different cards (see illustration on facing page).

Vitali, another intermediate-level English speaker whose native language is Russian, went next. Pointing to pairs of symbols at a time, he counted, "Two, four, six, eight, ten, twelve, fourteen, and one more is fifteen."

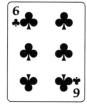 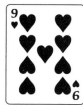

Because there wasn't a sentence frame to help Vitali explain his strategy, Christine asked the students what Vitali was doing to get the answer.

"Counting by twos!" several replied.

Christine then held up two more cards.

After giving the class time to solve the problem and whisper the answer aloud, Christine called on Solan to come up to the front of the rug.

"What answer did you get, Solan?" Christine asked.

"Thirteen, because seven and six is thirteen," she answered.

"How did you get thirteen?" Christine queried.

"I just knew it," Solan replied.

"So sometimes we just know what the answer is from memory," Christine commented. "But what if you didn't just know the answer right away—what would you do to figure it out?" Christine asked, pushing Solan for an explanation.

Pointing to the cards one at a time and using the sentence frames for support, Solan said, "First I start at seven and then I count on six more."

"So you could start at seven and count on six more," Christine paraphrased.

"How about another way to figure the answer?" Christine asked this question to send the message that there's often more than one way to solve a problem.

Ricardo, an advanced English learner, stepped to the front of the class and explained his reasoning. "I know my doubles. Seven plus seven is fourteen," he said, using one of the key vocabulary words in the lesson. "So I have to take away one, 'cause it's seven plus six. That makes thirteen." Christine was impressed with Ricardo's thinking.

Christine repeated Ricardo's strategy for the class. "So Ricardo knew that seven and seven is fourteen; then he subtracted or took away one to get thirteen."

Repeating, paraphrasing, or summarizing is an effective strategy because it gives English language learners another chance to hear and make sense of an idea. It also helps the teacher verify whether or not she has correctly understood a child's thinking.

Next, Christine held up a 10 and a 5:

Nester, an intermediate-level English learner, came up and stood next to Christine. Pointing first to the 10 and then to the 5, he said, "First I count ten, then I count five."

"Show us how you counted," Christine said.

Nester counted each of the ten hearts and then the five clubs to get a total of fifteen.

"Another way to figure the answer?" Christine probed.

"First I said ten, then I counted the five," Courtney reported.

After having the class find the sums of a few more pairs of cards, Christine brought an end to the lesson. *Capture* and *Double Capture* were math tasks that had encouraged and supported the development of oral language in English *and* had provided students with opportunities to develop more efficient strategies for combining numbers.

Modifications and Extensions

+ For kindergarten students, teach only the game of *Capture.*
+ When teaching *Capture*, change the rules so that a player wins if his number is *less than* his partner's number and change the sentence frame from _____ *is greater than* _____ to _____ *is less than* _____.
+ Teach only the game of *Double Capture.*
+ Teach the game of *Double Difference Capture.* In this version of the game, each player turns over two cards and the players

find the difference between their two numbers. Then the player with the smaller difference takes the cards. The player with the most cards at the end of the game is the winner.

Activity Directions ✦ **Capture and Double Capture**

Day 1

Minilesson Introducing Academic Language

1. Introduce playing cards to the class. Ask students to share what they already know or what they notice about a deck of cards. Be sure to point out the suits, the names and values of the cards, and how to shuffle and deal cards.

2. Model the game of *Capture* by playing with a student volunteer.

Directions for Capture

1. The dealer shuffles the cards and deals them one at a time, starting with his partner. Players place their cards in a pile facedown in front of them.

2. Each player takes the top card off his pile, turns it faceup, and announces its value.

3. Introduce the sentence frames:

> I have _____. You have _____.

> _____ is greater than _____.

4. The player with the card that has the greater number says, "_____ [the value of his card] is greater than _____ [the value of his opponent's card]," and takes both cards, creating a new capture pile.

5. If players turn over cards of equal value, each player takes back his own card and players continue with the next round. Introduce the word *equal* to students and the sentence frame:

> _____ is equal to _____.

Capture and Double Capture

31

6. Play continues until players have used all the cards in their original piles.

7. The winner is the player with the most cards in his capture pile.

Playing the Game

Distribute a deck of cards (with face cards removed) to each pair of students and have them play several games of *Capture*.

Day 2

Minilesson Introducing Academic Language

1. Introduce the name of the game to students, clarifying the meaning of the word *double* and adding the word to the vocabulary chart.

2. Model the game of *Double Capture* with a student volunteer. While modeling the game, introduce the following words and add them to the vocabulary chart: *add* and *plus, subtract* and *take away, count* and *counted.*

Directions *for* Double Capture

1. The dealer shuffles the cards and deals them one at a time, starting with her partner. Players place their cards in a pile facedown in front of them.

2. Each player takes the top two cards off her pile and turns them faceup. They then announce the value of each of their cards and add them together.

3. The player with the greater sum says, "I have _____. You have _____. _____ is greater than _____."

4. If players' sums are of equal value, they use the sentence frame and say, "_____ is equal to _____." Then each player takes back her own cards and they continue with the next round.

5. While you and the student volunteer play the game, model explaining different ways to combine the numbers on the cards. Elicit students'

ideas and introduce the following sentence frames to help students explain strategies:

First _____ , then _____ .

I know that _____ , so _____ .

6. Play continues until players have used all the cards in their original piles.

7. The winner is the player with the most cards in her capture pile.

Playing the Game

1. Distribute a deck of cards (with face cards removed) to each pair of students and have them play several games of *Double Capture*.

2. When students are finished playing, lead a class discussion. Hold up two cards at a time and ask the students to add the numbers together. Have students discuss how they combined the numbers, and encourage them to use the sentence frames for support.

3 From Rockets to Polygons

A Geometry Lesson

GRADE-LEVEL RECOMMENDATIONS

Day 1: Grades K, 1, and 2
Day 2: Grades 1 and 2

Overview

In this lesson, students cut a square into smaller pieces and then rearrange those pieces to reproduce a rocket shape. They then take the smaller pieces used to make the rocket and rearrange them to make a different polygon.

In a minilesson prior to the geometry lesson, students are introduced to vocabulary words and sentence frames that they will need in order to describe the rocket shape and the polygons that they create.

Math Goal: Identify, name, and describe common two-dimensional geometric shapes and their attributes

Language Goal: Describe objects

Key Vocabulary: angle(s), polygon(s), rectangle, side(s), square, triangle, vertex/vertices

Materials

+ $4\frac{1}{2}$-inch construction paper squares, 1 per student and 1 for the teacher
+ 1 piece of chart paper
+ 3 markers: 1 black, 1 red, and 1 blue
+ 6 sentence strips or pieces of construction paper for sentence frames

✦ 1 sheet of white construction paper for teacher's rocket design
✦ zip-top sandwich bags labeled with students' names, 1 per student

Sentence Frames That Help Students Describe Geometric Shapes

Beginning

A _____ has _____.

It has _____.

Intermediate and Advanced

A _____ has _____, _____, and _____.

My shape has _____, _____, and _____.

I built my shape with _____ and _____.

It looks like a _____.

Class Profile

Of the nineteen students in Kristin Burer's class, eleven are English language learners, including two beginning English speakers, eight intermediate English speakers, and one ELL with advanced fluency.

From the Classroom ✦ **Day 1: Rockets**

Minilesson Introducing Academic Language

The students in Kristin Burer's class sat in a circle on the rug, watching Kathy Melanese as she held up a $4\frac{1}{2}$-inch paper square for the students to see.

"Raise your hand if you know the name of this shape," Kathy directed. Lots of hands shot in the air. To tap their prior knowledge and to give all the students a chance to talk, Kathy had them turn to a partner and whisper the name of the shape. When they were finished, Kathy called on Jackie to name the shape.

"It's a square," Jackie announced.

"Thumbs up if you agree with Jackie," Kathy said. Everyone's thumb was turned up. Nonverbal responses help teachers check for understanding without requiring students to produce language. English language learners can participate and show that they understand a concept, or agree or disagree with someone's idea, without having to talk. This is especially important for students whose comprehension of English is more advanced than their ability to speak the language.

With a black marker, Kathy drew a square on a piece of chart paper that was taped to the board; she also wrote the word *square* next to the drawing. Kathy held up the paper square again and ran her index finger along the four sides.

"Think about the name of this part of the square," she said. Providing students individual think time gives them a chance to formulate their ideas. This is especially true of English learners.

"Now, turn to your partner and tell each other the name of this part of the square."

Kathy listened to a few students as they guessed. Some, like Joey, thought that it was the "line" of the square. But most students guessed correctly.

"So what do you think?" Kathy asked the class after she regained its attention.

"Side," Karyme responded. Karyme is a student with intermediate fluency in English.

On the class chart, Kathy wrote *side* next to one of the four sides in her sketch of the square.

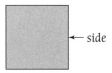 ← side

"How many sides are there on the square?" Kathy asked.

A few students called out "Four!" while some were busy trying to count the sides. Most did not respond to Kathy's question.

"Let's count the *sides* on the *square*," Kathy said, clearly enunciating each new vocabulary word. As Kathy ran her index finger along the four sides of the square, the students counted along with her.

Next, Kathy introduced the word *vertex* to the students. She told them that a vertex is the point where two sides join or come together. With a red marker, Kathy drew a little dot to illustrate each vertex on the square and wrote the word *vertex* on the chart. Using a different-colored marker than the black marker used for the sides helped the students make a distinction between the sides of the square and its vertices.

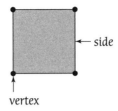

Kathy then asked for a volunteer to come up and touch a vertex on her paper square and a vertex on the square she'd drawn on the chart paper. As Christian touched each vertex, Kathy directed the students to say the word aloud in a choral voice. She then introduced the word *vertices*, wrote it on the class chart next to the word *vertex*, and explained to the students that *vertices* means more than one vertex.

"This is a vertex," Kathy said, pointing to the vertex on the paper square. Kathy directed the class to count the vertices aloud as she touched each vertex on her paper square.

"A square has four vertices," she stated, providing a context for the word's definition.

As with the sides and vertices, Kathy introduced the words *angle* and *angles* by drawing them in on the square on the class chart with a blue marker and writing the new vocabulary words on the chart.

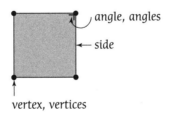

Once again, Kathy had a student volunteer come up and point to the angles on the square, and again she had the class count the angles and say the vocabulary word aloud in unison. Next, Kathy distributed one $4\frac{1}{2}$-inch paper square to each student.

"What's the name of this shape?" she asked.

"A square!" students responded with enthusiasm.

"Use your finger and point to the *sides* of your square," Kathy directed, saying the word *sides* in a slightly exaggerated tone. Kathy knows that modifying teacher talk can help English learners when they are being introduced to new terms.

Kathy continued, giving students practice using the new vocabulary words by having them point to the square's angles and vertices and saying the terms aloud. Then she introduced the first sentence frame by taping it to the board next to the class chart. Kathy wrote this frame in blue, color-coded for beginning-level English learners.

A _____ has _____.

Color-coding the sentence frames according to difficulty level makes it easier for students to differentiate between the frames. During a lesson, Kathy will sometimes suggest that a student use a particular frame that is more suited for him. Rather than having to say to a student, "I suggest that you use the frame for beginners," Kathy can refer to the frames by color and say something like, "Try the blue frame first."

"We can use this sentence frame to help us describe the square," Kathy told the class.

"For example, you could say, 'A square has four sides,'" she said, pointing to the words in the frame as she said them aloud. "Who would like to try?"

Adryana, an intermediate English speaker, volunteered. "A square has angles," she said.

Luis, a beginning English speaker, looked at the sentence frame and said, "A square has . . . ," then hesitated. Finally, after looking at the vocabulary chart, he said, "A square has angles." Although this was the same sentence that Adryana had offered, Kathy was pleased that a beginning English speaker like Luis would volunteer in front of the class.

"Let's all say Luis's sentence," Kathy told the class. Together, the students repeated Luis's description of the square.

Arianna went next. "A square has . . . ," she started and then hesitated. English learners sometimes need prompting to help them produce language.

"Can you use one of the numbers to describe the square?" Kathy asked.

After thinking for a few seconds, Arianna said, "A square has four vertices."

Once again, Kathy had the class practice Arianna's sentence. Then she directed partners to describe their squares using the sentence frame for help if they needed it. For younger children who are not yet reading, the sentence frames are used orally; the teacher models and the students repeat the frame.

As partners described their squares, Kathy made a quick lap around the circle of students. She listened in and noticed that everyone could produce sentences using the sentence frame for beginning English speakers:

- ✦ A square has four sides.
- ✦ A square has sides.
- ✦ A square has four vertices.
- ✦ A square has vertices.
- ✦ A square has four angles.
- ✦ A square has angles.

After partners had practice using the beginning sentence frame, Kathy regained the students' attention by giving a series of directions.

"If you can hear me, put your hands on your head," she began. She continued, "If you can hear me, point to a vertex on your square. Now point to an angle. Point to a side." Kathy is always looking for ways to incorporate content while managing student behavior. In this case, she focused the students' attention by engaging them with the new vocabulary words they were learning.

Once Kathy had their complete attention, she introduced a sentence frame for intermediate and advanced ELLs, color-coded in red, by taping it to the board underneath the beginning frame:

Pointing to the sentence frame, Kathy said, "A square has . . ."

She counted aloud the blank spaces that were remaining in the frame. "The blank spaces mean to tell three things about the square," Kathy said to the class. "Who thinks you can use this frame to describe the square?"

After several seconds of wait time, Kathy called on Andrés, an English learner with intermediate fluency.

"A square has vertices, angles, and sides," he said.

"A square has angles and vertices," Arianna chimed in, using part of the frame. English learners will often either use sentence frames that are appropriate to their language level or, when the frame is too difficult, use the part of the frame that makes sense to them.

"A square has four angles and vertices," Xtlalli, an intermediate-level English speaker, offered. Like Arianna, Xtlalli used two rather than three descriptors.

"A . . . got square have four . . . ," Bryant, a beginning-level English speaker, began. Using an intermediate-level sentence frame was a challenge for him, but Kathy waited and gave him a chance to stretch his skills.

After pausing, Bryant successfully self-corrected and said, "The square have four sides." Bryant not only self-corrected but self-regulated as well. He realized that the intermediate sentence frame was too difficult, so he went back and used the beginning frame. Kathy did not correct his grammatical error (*have* rather than *has*). Although she often gives students explicit feedback when they make grammatical errors, in this case Kathy was satisfied that Bryant's second attempt was an improvement over his first sentence.

Luis, the other beginning English speaker in the class, contributed the next sentence. "A square has four sides, four angles, and, hmmm, four vertices," he said. Kathy was impressed that Luis used the intermediate frame, challenging himself and stretching his English language skills.

To bring an end to the minilesson, Kathy had the students practice describing their squares using the new sentence frame. The minilesson had introduced the students to new vocabulary as well as to sentence frames that were designed to help them use the vocabulary to describe geometric shapes. The students seemed ready for the main part of the math lesson.

Making Rockets

To begin the geometry lesson, Kathy distributed a pair of scissors to each student. She then used the following directions to model for them how to fold and cut their square to make four shapes—a rectangle, a large triangle, and two small triangles:

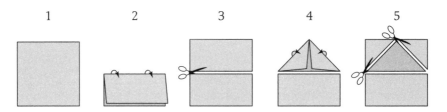

Most of the students in the class were able to fold and cut their squares with little difficulty. For some, however, it was a challenge. Kathy made her way around the circle of students, helping when needed and encouraging students to help one another. When they were finished folding and cutting, Kathy directed the students to place their shapes in front of them on the rug.

"Take a look at the shapes you've made," she said.

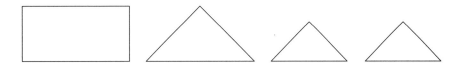

"Does anyone know the names of the four shapes? What about this shape?" Kathy asked, holding up the rectangle.

"Rectangle! It's a rectangle!" several students called out.

"And this shape?" Kathy asked, holding up the large triangle. Most students knew the name of the shape. Kathy continued, holding up each of the small triangles for the students to identify. As they said the name of each shape, Kathy drew a sketch of it on the class chart, wrote the name next to the drawing, and labeled each shape's sides, vertices, and angles. She then gave the class about two minutes to explore the shapes they'd made.

The students immediately began putting the shapes together in different ways. Kathy observed the students, asking several of them to talk to her about their designs. Providing contexts for English learners to have discussions in math class is important; giving them something purposeful and motivating to talk about is crucial.

"I made an arrow that's pointing down," Andrés said.

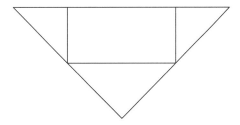

Adryana, another intermediate-level English learner, described her shape by saying, "I made an arrow pointing up, an arrow pointing down, and an arrow pointing that way," and gesturing to the right.

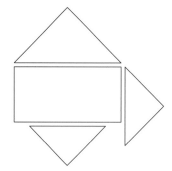

"I made a house with windows," Antonio explained.

"A tree, a triangle, and a rectangle," Mae described.

Kristal, a native English speaker, said, "I used two triangles to make a bow."

As students finished exploring with their shapes, Kathy quickly collected the scissors and then counted down from ten to regain the students' attention. She instructed them to put their shapes on the floor in front of them.

"Show me the rectangle," Kathy directed. The students picked up their rectangles to show that they knew the name and the shape.

"How many triangles do you have?" Kathy inquired.
Students instantly knew and called back, "Three!"

Kathy then picked up one of the small triangles, holding it like this:

"A triangle always has how many sides?" she asked the class.

Although most students knew the answer, Kathy had them run their fingers along each of the three sides of one of their triangles to verify.

"Let's practice saying that," Kathy said. "A triangle always has three sides."

The students echoed back the sentence in a choral voice. Echo talk can be an effective strategy for giving students practice with producing language and learning grammatically correct ways to formulate sentences.

Kathy then rotated the triangle she was holding so that it looked like this:

"Is it still a triangle?" she asked the class. Kathy asked this question because young children often hold the misconception that for a shape to be a triangle, it must rest on a plane in a certain fashion. They have a similar misconception about squares. Once a square is rotated a bit, children will often call it a diamond and think it's different than a square.

There was a mix of opinions. Some thought that the triangle was still a triangle, while others disagreed. Kathy confirmed that the shape was still a triangle, no matter how she shifted it.

Next, Kathy showed the students a rocket she had made by gluing down the four shapes on a piece of white construction paper:

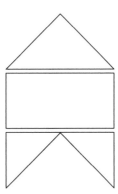

When Kathy told the students that they were to copy her design and make a rocket from their four shapes, they became animated. Soon, students were busy moving their shapes around to make their own rocket designs.

"I made it!" students shouted with excitement. Everyone was able to make the rocket design.

When all of the students had made their rockets, Kathy asked for their attention and focused them on the rocket that she had made, now taped to the board. With a black marker, she traced the sides of the rocket shape as the students counted the six sides. She then used a red marker to make dots for the six vertices on the rocket shape. Again, Kathy directed the students to count the vertices in a choral voice. Finally, she used a blue marker to denote the six angles.

Next, Kathy directed the students to describe their rockets to a partner, using the sentence frames if they needed them.

"The rocket has six sides," Joey, an intermediate English speaker, said.

Using the intermediate and advanced frame for support, Jaqueline said, "The rocket has six vertices, six sides, and six angles."

"There are six of everything!" Christian reported. Kathy was impressed with his observation.

To bring the lesson to a close for the day, Kathy distributed a zip-top bag to each student. Each bag had a student's name written on it with marker. To assess students' ability to identify each shape by name, Kathy gave specific directions for putting the shapes into the bags.

"Put the *large triangle* in your bag," Kathy told them, emphasizing the words *large* and *triangle*. "Now put the *small triangles* in your bag. Finally, put the *rectangle* away."

✦ Day 2: From Rockets to Polygons

To continue the lesson, Kathy called the students to the rug and distributed their bags. She then directed them to take their shapes out of their bags and gave them a few minutes to explore making designs. After a couple of minutes, she asked for their attention and addressed the class.

"Who can describe the square for us?" Kathy asked, pointing to the square she'd drawn on the class chart.

"A square has sides," Andrés said.

"A square has vertices," Kayla added.

"And it has four angles," Christian offered.

"Let's talk about the other shapes," Kathy said. "Hold up your rectangle. How many sides, angles, and vertices does it have? Talk with a partner."

As partners shared, Kathy quickly checked to see if they needed help using the sentence frames, paying close attention to students with beginning English skills and students who are nonreaders or beginning readers. After partners were finished, Kathy had volunteers come up and point to and count the sides, vertices, and angles of the rectangle drawn on the class chart.

"What do you notice about the rectangle and the square?" Kathy asked. She waited a few seconds to let students think about her open-ended question. When no one raised a hand, Kathy asked a more focused question. "How many sides are there on a rectangle?" she asked.

"Four!" students chorused.

"They're the same as the square!" Christian noticed. "The square has four sides and the rectangle does, too!"

"But they are shorter," Andrés added. "The rectangle has two short lines."

"The rectangle has two short sides," Kathy paraphrased, inserting correct terminology and pointing to the short sides of the rectangle to provide visual support. Kathy urged Andrés to echo her words, correcting his observation.

"The square and the rectangle have four things," Mae announced.

"Four what?" Kathy probed.

"Sides and angles," Mae responded.

"And vertexes!" Roman added.

"Yes, both shapes have vertices," Kathy corrected, careful to acknowledge Roman's contribution, but also to make sure he learned the correct usage. "Let's use the longer sentence frame to add onto Mae's and Roman's observations."

Kathy pointed to the intermediate and advanced frame from the previous day and had the students use it aloud in unison, following her lead. Kathy modeled the sentence first, then the students followed. "A square and a rectangle have four sides, four vertices, and four angles."

Kathy added an observation herself, noting with a light touch that a square is a special type of rectangle whose sides and angles are all the same.

After having the students describe the features of the triangles using the sentence frames for support, Kathy gave instructions for the next part of the lesson.

"Next, you are going to go back to your desks and use your shapes to make a new shape or design," Kathy explained. "You're going to put your shapes together to make a polygon, a shape with many sides." Kathy wrote the word *polygon* on the class chart to add to the vocabulary list.

"The triangle is a polygon with three sides, and the rectangle and square are polygons with how many sides?"

"Four!" several students chorused.

Kathy used Alexis's shapes to model how to put them together to make a new polygon. She told the students that when making a new shape or polygon, they would have to follow these rules:

1. The sides that touch have to be the same length.
2. You cannot put a shape on top of another shape.
3. You can use two, three, or four shapes to make a new shape.

Kathy made sure that she showed examples of shapes that were OK and ones that were not OK.

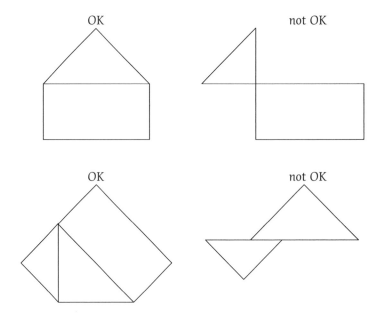

"When you go back to your seat, make several new shapes," Kathy continued. "Once you find a shape or polygon you like, check in with me first, and then glue it onto a piece of paper."

When she was finished repeating the directions, Kathy dismissed the students to their seats and distributed glue and paper. As they worked, Kathy circulated around the room, providing assistance as needed. After each student finished making a new shape, Kathy checked to make sure all of the rules had been followed. When a student had her new shape glued down, Kathy took a black marker and traced the sides of the shape, directing the student to count the sides along with her. Tracing the polygons made it easier for students to identify the correct number of sides.

Describing the Polygons

After about fifteen minutes, Kathy called the students to the rug with their new shapes. When the class was assembled, she introduced four new sentence frames to support students in describing their shapes. This first frame, color-coded in blue, was for beginning English learners:

It has _____.

The following three frames, color-coded in red, were intended for intermediate and advanced English language learners:

My shape has _____, _____, and _____.

I built my shape with _____ and _____.

It looks like a _____.

Kathy taped the new frames to the board and had the students practice saying them, pausing for the blank spaces. Then she asked for a volunteer to bring his or her new shape or polygon up to the front and show it to the class. Alexis, a native English speaker, went first. She had put the four pieces back together to make the original square.

Using two of the frames for support, Alexis said, "My shape has four sides, four angles, and four vertices. It looks like a square." (See Figure 3–1.)

Kathy had the class repeat Alexis's description. Then she called on Joey, an English learner with intermediate fluency. He stood in front of the class and held up his paper. Joey had re-created the rocket design.

"It has four sides," Joey said.

"Are you sure?" Kathy asked. "Count the sides again."

After counting, Joey corrected himself by saying, "It has six sides."

FIGURE 3-1.
Alexis put
the shapes
back together
to make a
square.

"Who can use the second frame to describe your shape?" Kathy asked, pointing to the sentence frame. Mark brought his paper to the front. He'd made a large triangle using the four pieces.

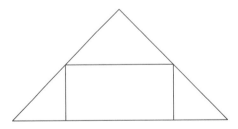

"I built my shape with three triangles and a rectangle," he said, using part of the frame.

When Mark was finished, Kathy instructed the students to describe their new shapes with a partner, using the sentence frames for support. As they shared, Kathy listened in.

"My shape looks like a rocket," Ricardo, a native English speaker, described. "It has six sides, six angles, and six vertices."

Mae used the most basic sentence frame from the previous day's lesson and said, "It has five vertices."

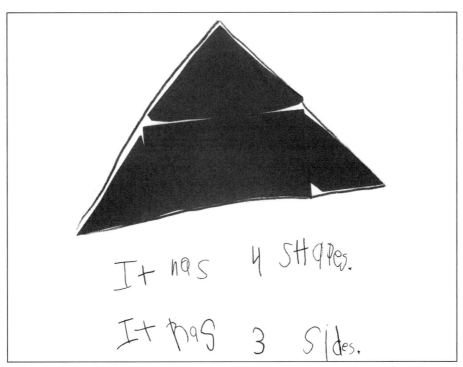

It has 4 shapes.

It has 3 sides.

FIGURE 3-2.
Isaiah's
triangle.

Isaiah described the triangle he made by saying, "It has four shapes. It has three sides." (See Figure 3–2.)

Joscelyne said, "It looks like a house. It has five sides. It has five vertices." (See Figure 3–3.)

"It looks like a pointer," Andrés said, describing the large triangle he had made using all four shapes.

"It looks like a shoe," said Adryana. "It has five sides." (See Figure 3–4.)

As Kathy listened to the students describe their polygons, she knew that the explicit vocabulary instruction, the support that the sentence frames provided, and the repeated opportunities for practice in meaningful contexts in the lesson had all contributed to the students' language development. She also recognized that the students would need further experience over time in order to develop their ability to effectively communicate about geometric figures in English.

To finish the lesson, Kathy sent the students back to their desks and had them write about their new shapes, providing them with further experience using language to learn about geometric shapes and using geometry as a context for developing their English language skills. (See Figure 3–5.)

From Rockets to Polygons

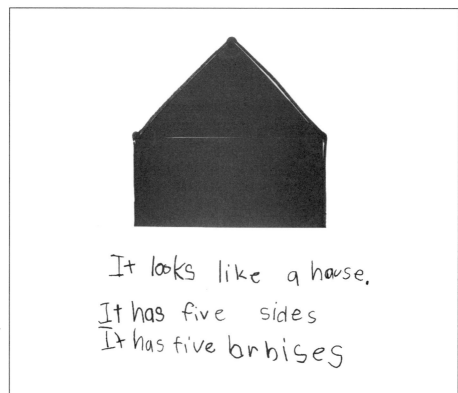

It looks like a house.
It has five sides
It has five brbises

FIGURE 3-3. Joscelyne made a pentagon using two shapes.

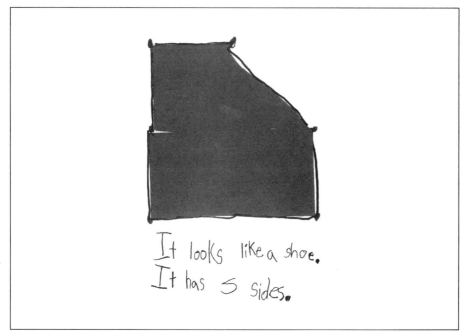

It looks like a shoe.
It has 5 sides.

FIGURE 3-4. Adryana said her pentagon looked like a shoe.

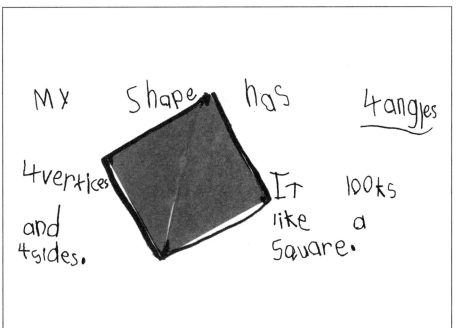

My Shape has 4 angles

4 vertices and 4 sides.

It looks like a square.

FIGURE 3-5. Cristian used lots of language to describe his square.

Modifications for Younger Children

◆ Teach the lesson in small groups.
◆ Teach only Day 1 of the lesson.
◆ Teach Day 1 of the lesson in a whole-group setting, and then teach Day 2 of the lesson in small groups.
◆ Use the sentence frames orally, especially for children who are not yet able to read.

Extensions

◆ Introduce the names of the various polygons that students make and expect students to use the names when describing their polygons:

Possible polygons:

Triangle

Quadrilateral

Pentagon

Hexagon

◆ Ask students to describe the geometric shapes they see inside the polygon they made.

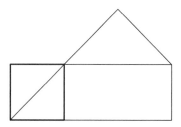

"I see a square inside the hexagon."

Activity Directions ◆ **From Rockets to Polygons**

Day I

Minilesson Introducing Academic Language

1. Show the students a $4\frac{1}{2}$-inch paper square. Ask them to identify the shape. If none of the students are familiar with the term *square*, tell them the name and have them repeat it. Draw and label a square on a piece of chart paper.

2. Hold up the paper square and trace your finger along the sides, saying the word *side* aloud to the students. Have them repeat the word. Label a side of the square drawn on the chart paper. Touching each side of the square, count the number of sides aloud with the students.

3. Introduce the word *vertex* in the same manner by pointing to the vertices on the square and saying the word aloud. Have students repeat the words *vertex* and *vertices*. Label a vertex on the chart. Together with the students, count the number of vertices on the square. Continue with the same procedure for the words *angle* and *angles*.

4. Distribute a $4\frac{1}{2}$-inch paper square to each student. Ask them to name the shape and have them show you the sides, vertices, and angles using their own squares. Introduce the beginning sentence frame and have students practice, pausing for the blank spaces:

A _____ has _____ .

With the sentence frame for support, direct students to describe their square using the vocabulary words *sides*, *vertices*, and *angles*.

5. Introduce the intermediate and advanced sentence frame, directing the students to practice saying it, pausing for the blank spaces.

A _____ has _____, _____, and _____.

With the sentence frame for support, direct students to describe their square using the vocabulary words.

Making Rockets

1. Distribute a pair of scissors to each student. Model how to fold and cut the square to make two small triangles, one large triangle, and a rectangle. After students have made all of the shapes, ask them to identify each one and add the names to the chart, labeling the sides, vertices, and angles.

2. Give students about two minutes to explore and talk about their new shapes.

3. Collect the scissors and have students put their shapes in front of them. Show the students a completed model of a rocket shape that you made prior to class:

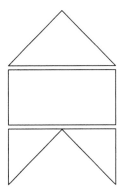

Direct the students to use their shapes to make the rocket.

4. With a black marker, trace the sides of the rocket shape you made as a model. Together with the students, count the sides. Using a red marker, make dots for the rocket's vertices, and together with the students, count them. Use a blue marker to denote the rocket's angles and count them aloud with the students.

5. Direct the students to describe their rockets using the vocabulary introduced and the sentence frames.

6. Have each student put his shapes in a zip-top bag, which you have labeled with his name.

Day 2

From Rockets to Polygons

1. Hand back students' shapes and give them a few minutes to explore. When they're finished, ask students to describe their shapes.

2. Introduce the vocabulary word *polygon*. Model how to make a polygon from the shapes students have: two small triangles, one large triangle, and a rectangle.

3. Review the rules for making a polygon:

- ✦ The sides that touch have to match.
- ✦ You cannot put a shape on top of another shape.
- ✦ You can use two, three, or four shapes to make a new shape.
- ✦ Once you make a shape, check with the teacher, then glue it down on a piece of paper.

4. Distribute paper and glue and direct students to make polygons.

5. When students are finished making their polygons, begin a class discussion by introducing the following sentence frames:

It has _____.

My shape has _____ , _____ , and _____ .

I built my shape with _____ and _____ .

It looks like a _____.

6. Have the students use the sentence frames and the vocabulary introduced to describe their polygons.

7. Direct the students to write about their polygons.

Trade Up for a Nickel, Trade Up for a Dime, and Race for a Quarter 4

Number Sense Lessons About Money

GRADE-LEVEL RECOMMENDATIONS

Trade Up for a Nickel and *Trade Up for a Dime:* Grades K and 1
Race for a Quarter: Grades 1 and 2

Overview
In these lessons, students play games that help them learn the names and values of coins and how to trade for coins of equal value. Students are introduced to sentence frames that can be used for all three games. The frames help the students describe quantities of money and tell how to make trades.

Math Goal: Identify and know the value of coins; show different combinations of coins that equal the same value

Language Goal: Describe quantities; explain cause and effect when trading for coins of equal value

Key Vocabulary: cents, dime, money, nickel, penny, quarter, trade

Materials for *Trade Up for a Nickel*

✦ vocabulary word cards for *cents, trade, penny, nickel*
✦ pocket chart
✦ decks of *Trade Up for a Nickel* amount cards, 1 per pair or small group of students (see Blackline Masters)
✦ *Trade Up for a Nickel* game boards, 1 per student (see Blackline Masters)
✦ zip-top sandwich bags each containing 15 pennies and 5 nickels (real coins are best), 1 per student
✦ 3 sentence strips for sentence frames

Materials for *Trade Up for a Dime*

✦ zip-top sandwich bags each containing 15 pennies and 5 dimes (real coins are best), 1 per student
✦ *Trade Up for a Dime* game boards, 1 per student (see Blackline Masters)
✦ decks of *Trade Up for a Dime* amount cards, 1 per pair or small group of students (see Blackline Masters)
✦ 3 sentence strips for sentence frames
✦ vocabulary word cards for *cents, trade, penny, nickel, dime*
✦ pocket chart

Materials for *Race for a Quarter*

✦ 1 piece of white construction paper
✦ vocabulary word cards for *cents, trade, penny, nickel, dime, quarter*
✦ zip-top sandwich bags each containing 30 pennies, 10 nickels, 10 dimes, and 1 quarter (real coins are best), 1 per pair of students
✦ dice, 1 per pair of students
✦ 3 sentence strips for sentence frames
✦ rules for *Race for a Quarter*, 1 copy per pair of students (see Blackline Masters)
✦ *A Quarter from the Tooth Fairy*, by Caren Holtzman (Scholastic 1995)

Sentence Frames That Help Students Describe Quantities of Money and Explain How They Can Make a Trade

Beginning

> *I need* _____ *more* _____ .

> I have _____ , so I need _____ more _____ .

> I have _____ , so I can trade for _____ .

✦ **Trade Up for a Nickel**

Class Profile

Of the nineteen students in Diana Whitaker's class, twelve are English language learners (ELLs). Six students have beginning English language skills, two are students with intermediate fluency, and four students have advanced fluency. English, Spanish, and Tagalog are the native languages spoken by the students.

Working with Small Groups

The students in Diana Whitaker's class had just finished their morning meeting and were dismissed to work in small groups at learning centers. Kathy Melanese sat down on the front rug to work with a small group of four students; eventually, Kathy would get a chance to work with all of the students during the math period.

Because she had only about fifteen minutes to work with her group before they rotated to the next center, Kathy decided to introduce key vocabulary and sentence frames in the context of the activity rather than in a minilesson prior to the game of *Trade Up for a Nickel*.

Kathy's group consisted of Marshe, who is a native English speaker; Nelia, a student with intermediate proficiency in English; and Josh and Diego, who both have beginning-level skills in English. Kathy started out the lesson by tapping the students' prior knowledge, asking them what they knew about money.

"You can spend money," Nelia said.

"You can buy stuff," Josh added.

"You can buy groceries from the store!" Marshe exclaimed.

"You can buy food that you need," Diego said.

"How do you buy food that you need?" Kathy asked the group.

"With dollars!" they responded.

"I don't have a dollar to show you," Kathy told the students. "But I do have this coin." Kathy held up a penny and asked the students if they knew the name of the coin. All four students correctly identified the penny.

"How much is a penny worth?" Kathy asked. When no one responded, Kathy held up a word card with the word *cents* and its symbol written on it. She had the students practice saying the word aloud and then inserted the card in a pocket chart near the students. Kathy also held up a card with a picture of a penny on it, its name, and the corresponding value and placed it in the pocket chart.

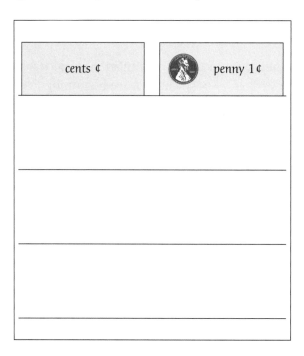

"How much is a penny worth?" Kathy asked, holding up the coin and pointing to the card in the chart.

"One cent!" the students responded. Kathy directed the students to say, "A penny is worth one cent," together in a choral voice. First she modeled the sentence, and then she had the students echo back.

Next, Kathy held up a nickel and asked the students if they knew the name of the coin. This time, no one in the group could identify the coin's name. These students hadn't been formally taught about money prior to the lesson.

After she told the students that the coin was called a nickel, she asked, "How much do you think a nickel is worth?"

"Twenty-five cents?" Nelia guessed.

When no one else had a guess, Kathy told the students that a nickel is worth five cents. As with the penny, Kathy held up a card with a picture of a nickel on it, its name, and its corresponding value and slipped the card into the pocket chart.

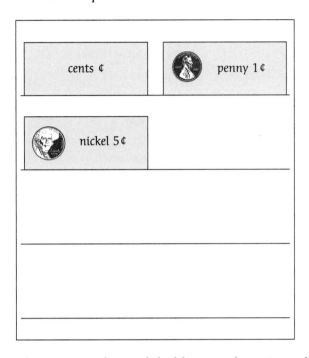

"Repeat after me," Kathy said, holding up the coin and pointing to the *nickel* and *cents* cards in the pocket chart. "A nickel is worth five cents." The students responded in a choral voice.

"Show me with your fingers how many *cents* a *penny* is worth," Kathy directed, exaggerating the key vocabulary words. She held up one finger to model, and then all four students followed suit. Kathy did the same for the nickel, holding up five fingers to stand for how many cents a nickel is worth, and the students again copied her. Kathy repeated this over and over to give the students practice.

Kathy then showed the students a deck of amount cards (twenty cards in all); each card had one of the following amounts written on it: 1¢, 2¢, or 3¢.

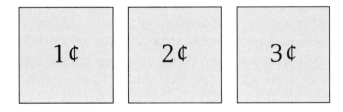

As she held up each card, Kathy had the students say aloud how many cents the card was worth.

Next, Kathy distributed a *Trade Up for a Nickel* game board to each student in the group.

Once the students had their game boards, Kathy gave each student a plastic zip-top sandwich bag; in each bag there were fifteen pennies and five nickels. Kathy had the students empty the contents of their bags next to their game boards and sort their coins into piles of pennies and piles of nickels.

"Point to the pennies," Kathy directed. "Now point to the nickels." Kathy likes to include questions and prompts in her lessons that require students to *show* as well as *tell*. This gives students with beginning English language skills a chance to participate without having to produce language.

Next, Kathy had the children count the nickels they had in their collection and then count how many pennies they had. She was interested in how high the students could count in English, and if they were able to tag each coin and say the number simultaneously, demonstrating whether or not they had one-to-one correspondence. Although it is helpful when playing *Trade Up for a Nickel* if students know how to count up to at least five (and count up to ten for the extension, *Trade Up for a Dime*), the game can give students experience and practice *learning* how to count.

Playing the Game

When the students were finished counting their coins, Kathy was ready to begin playing the game with the group. To start, she called on Marshe to pull an amount card from the deck. Marshe selected a card that was labeled 3¢ and held it up for the rest of the group to see.

"What amount is on the card?" Kathy asked.

"Three!" the students shot back.

"Three cents," Kathy added, pointing to the word *cents* in the pocket chart to reinforce this new vocabulary word. She had the students repeat after her.

"Three cents!" the students called back.

"Whatever shows on the amount card, that's how many pennies you put on your *Trade Up for a Nickel* game board," Kathy explained. "Get three pennies and put one penny in each box."

All four students easily placed three pennies on their game board. Putting a penny in each box helps students develop the idea of one-to-one correspondence: one penny to each box. Kathy also had a game board of her own with which to model, and she made sure that students knew to place their pennies in the boxes, one next to the other without skipping boxes.

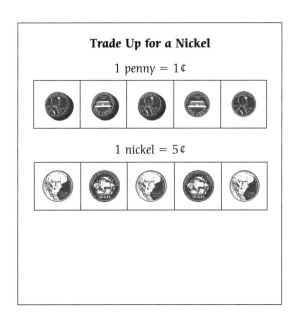

"How many pennies are there on our board right now?" Kathy asked. "Show me with your fingers." All the students held up three fingers to show the amount.

"How many *more* pennies do you need to have five pennies?" Kathy asked the group.

"Two!" Nelia exclaimed.

"Show us how you know," Kathy said. Nelia pointed to the two empty boxes on her *Trade Up for a Nickel* game board.

"So we can say that we need two more pennies," Kathy told the group. She placed the following sentence frame for beginning English learners into the pocket chart:

> *I need* _____ *more* _____ *.*

"Repeat after me," Kathy said. "I need two more pennies!"

"I need two more pennies!" the students echoed back.

"We could also say, 'I have three pennies, so I need two more pennies,'" Kathy said, as she placed a more advanced sentence frame in the pocket chart:

> *I have* _____ *, so I need* _____ *more* _____ *.*

"Repeat after me," Kathy told the group. "I have three pennies, so I need two more to trade for a nickel." With some help from Kathy, the students repeated her sentence. Kathy used the sentence frames in the pocket chart more as a reference for herself. Children who are reading independently can read the sentence frames, but for younger children, Kathy uses the frames orally; she reads them aloud and then has the children echo the words back.

Next, Kathy had Diego choose an amount card from the deck, hold it up for the students to see, and tell what was on the card.

"There's one cent," Diego observed.

The students placed another penny on their game board. Kathy asked them how many pennies were on their game board; she also asked them to show with their fingers how many more pennies they would need to have five pennies.

"Let's practice," Kathy said. "Repeat after me. I need one more penny."

"I need one more penny!" the students responded.

"Or we could say, 'I have four pennies, so I need one more penny.'"

The students echoed back Kathy's sentence. Kathy's goal was for students to begin to use the language in the sentence frames more independently as they gained practice with the game of *Trade Up for a Nickel*.

Josh drew the next amount card, which showed 2¢.

"Do we have enough boxes to fit two pennies?" Kathy asked.

"There's only one box left," Marshe observed.

"We have to have exactly five pennies to trade for a nickel," Kathy told the group. "So we have to draw another card; we don't want to have any leftover pennies."

Josh drew the next amount card, which showed 1¢. The students each placed a penny on their game board.

"How many pennies do we have now?" Kathy asked.

"Five!" the students replied.

"Are you sure? Count them to make sure," Kathy urged the group. As the students counted, Kathy placed the word card *trade* in the pocket chart. She pointed to the word and had the students say it aloud.

"What do you think *trade* means?" Kathy asked the group.

"It means you give something and that person gives you something back," Marshe explained.

"That's right," Kathy acknowledged. "If you give me five pennies, then I would give you a nickel because a nickel is worth five pennies, or five cents. We would *trade* five pennies for a nickel." As Kathy said the word *trade*, she gestured, moving her open palms back and forth to illustrate the word.

"Do we have enough pennies to make a trade for a nickel?" Kathy asked. This question stumped the children, so Kathy rephrased it. "How many pennies make a nickel?"

"Five!"

"Do we have five pennies to trade for a nickel?"

This time, the students' knowing nods revealed their understanding. Kathy modeled how to take her hand and carefully sweep off the row of five pennies, place them on the carpet, and replace them or trade them by putting a nickel in the single box at the beginning of the row underneath (see illustration on next page).

Kathy placed the last sentence frame in the pocket chart:

I have _____ , so I can trade for _____ .

Pointing to the words in the sentence frame, intended for intermediate and advanced English learners, Kathy modeled for the group. "We can say, 'I have five cents, so I can trade for a nickel.'"

Kathy had the students repeat this as they swept the pennies off their game board and replaced them with a nickel.

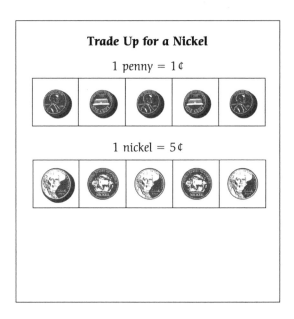

Trade Up for a Nickel

1 penny = 1¢

1 nickel = 5¢

Kathy continued to play the game of *Trade Up for a Nickel* with the small group of students. As they played, she asked the same questions over and over and had the students use the sentence frames and the key vocabulary to answer them:

- ✦ How many pennies do you have on your game board?
- ✦ How many more pennies or cents do you need to trade for a nickel?

After the students had filled up their game board with five nickels, Kathy helped them count the nickels by fives to twenty-five. To finish up, Kathy reviewed the names and values of the pennies and nickels and then had the students put the coins away in their zip-top bags, ready for the next small group.

Extending the Lesson: Trade Up for a Dime

After Kathy played *Trade Up for a Nickel* with the rest of the small groups in the class, she left for the day. On subsequent days, Diana Whitaker played *Trade Up for a Nickel* with her students until she felt that they were ready for *Trade Up for a Dime*.

In this game, each student needs five dimes and fifteen pennies and a *Trade Up for a Dime* game board. Instead of trading for a nickel when they get five pennies, students trade for a dime when they get ten pennies. When all ten dimes are collected, students count how many dimes they have altogether and then count by tens to one dollar.

For *Trade Up for a Dime*, the students use amount cards that each have one of the following amounts written on them: 1¢, 2¢, 3¢, 4¢, or 5¢. Diana Whitaker also used the same sentence frames from *Trade Up for a Nickel* as well as vocabulary word cards to help students describe quantities of money and to help them explain how they could make a trade.

✦ Race for a Quarter

Class Profile

Of the twenty students in Shawn Yoshimoto's class, half are native English speakers, and the other half are English learners with intermediate and advanced fluency in English. The English language learners in Shawn's class speak Spanish as their native language.

Minilesson to Introduce Academic Language

When Kathy Melanese visited Shawn Yoshimoto's class, she had the students gather in a circle on the rug in the front of the room. As she did with the children in Diana Whitaker's class, Kathy tapped the students' prior knowledge about money by placing a penny, a dime, a nickel, and a quarter on a white piece of construction paper in the middle of the circle of children. She asked the students to turn to a partner and talk about the names and values of the coins. When they were finished, she had volunteers identify the coins' names and values. After that, Kathy posted word cards on the board with the pictures, names, and values of the coins. As she did this, Kathy directed the students to say the names and values of the coins aloud several times.

Word Cards

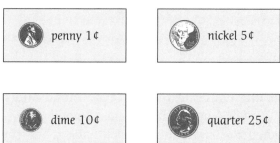

To model how to play the game, Kathy chose Amanda, a student with intermediate fluency in English, to play a game with her.

"We're going to play a game called *Race for a Quarter*," Kathy told the class. "I'm going to play against Amanda. We'll take turns rolling the die. Whatever comes up on the die, that's how many pennies to take. The first person to get twenty-five cents is the winner."

Kathy held up a zip-top sandwich bag that had a collection of thirty pennies, ten nickels, ten dimes, and one quarter inside. "This will be Amanda's and my bank where we get the coins to play the game."

The students were excited to learn the game. Games can provide rich and safe contexts for discussing math ideas, and they serve to motivate and engage all students, including English language learners.

Kathy went first and rolled a 3 on the die. "What do I do now?" Kathy asked the class.

"Take three pennies!" several students exclaimed. Kathy took three pennies from the sandwich bag and placed them on a piece of white construction paper so that all the students could see.

Amanda went next and rolled a 2; she took two pennies from the same sandwich bag.

"Let's take a look at *my* pennies," Kathy said to the class as she pointed to her coins. "How much money do I have?"

"Three cents!" the students shot back.

"How much do I need to trade or exchange for a nickel?" Kathy asked as she placed the word card *trade* on the board and had the students say the word aloud several times. Kathy likes to use synonyms for key words (e.g., *exchange* for *trade*) to help English learners comprehend and extend their vocabulary.

"Two more pennies!" Joel exclaimed.

Kathy placed the sentence frame for beginning English learners on the board and had the class practice reading it aloud, pausing for the blank spaces.

I need _____ more _____.

Pointing to the words in the sentence frame and the word card *pennies*, Kathy modeled using the frame. "I need two more pennies." Then she directed the students to echo back what she said several times.

Pointing to the word card *cents*, Kathy said, "Or we could say, 'I have three cents, so I need two more to trade for a nickel.'" She then placed the intermediate and advanced sentence frame on the board and had the students practice using it several times:

> I have _____ , so I need _____ more _____.

After the students were finished practicing the frame, Amanda took her turn. She rolled a 1 on the die.

"How much money do you have, Amanda?" Kathy asked her.

"I have three cents," Amanda replied.

"How much more do you need to make a trade?" Kathy asked.

Using the sentence frames and vocabulary word cards for support, Amanda said, "I have three cents, so I need two more pennies."

Kathy directed the students to repeat what Amanda said, giving them further practice using the sentence frame. When the class was finished, Kathy rolled the die again; this time she rolled another 3 and took three pennies from the sandwich bag. Now she had six pennies.

"What do I do now?" Kathy asked the class.

"Trade!" the students responded.

"Remind me what the word *trade* means," Kathy said, as she pointed to the word card on the board.

"It's like if someone gives you something and you give something back to them," Raymond explained.

"How many pennies do I trade for a nickel?" Kathy asked.

"Five, 'cause a nickel is worth five cents," Farah noted. "They're equal, they're worth the same."

Kathy took five of her pennies and traded it in for one nickel. Then she put the final sentence frame on the board and had the students practice reading it, pausing for the blank spaces:

> I have _____ , so I can trade for a _____.

"Let's practice using the frame," Kathy instructed. She went first and then had the students echo back, "I have five pennies, so I can trade for a nickel."

After the students repeated Kathy's sentence, Oscar raised his hand and said, "You really have six pennies, but you can trade five of them for a nickel."

"That's correct," Kathy acknowledged. "I'll keep the penny that's left over, so I have one nickel and one penny."

Kathy and Amanda continued to model the game for the class. After each turn, Kathy asked the class two questions and then had the students use the sentence frames to respond:

✦ How much money do I have? How do you know?
✦ How much more do I need to make a trade?

After a few more turns, Kathy had one dime, one nickel, and three pennies in front of her:

"How much money do I have?" Kathy asked. "Think about it for a few seconds, and then turn to a partner and talk about how you figured the answer."

When conversations died down, Kathy asked for a few volunteers to explain their thinking. Terrance, a native English speaker, went first.

"There's eighteen cents. I know that 'cause ten plus five is fifteen cents," he began. "And then I counted the three pennies: sixteen, seventeen, and eighteen."

Carmen, an English learner with intermediate fluency, explained, "It's eighteen cents. I did five and three is eight. And then eight plus ten is eighteen cents."

"Did anyone figure it a different way than Terrance and Carmen?" Kathy asked the class.

Alberto, a student with advanced fluency in English, said, "I started with the dime and then [pointing to the nickel] went eleven, twelve, thirteen, fourteen, fifteen."

Alberto paused to think, then pointed to the pennies and continued counting, "Sixteen, seventeen, eighteen."

Working with money can provide a rich context for combining quantities in different ways. While Kathy eventually wants students to figure the total amount of a mixed collection of coins in efficient ways (e.g., starting with the largest amounts), she also values the different ways that the students reason. Most importantly, she wants the children to be able to communicate their math thinking in English.

"So I have eighteen cents," Kathy confirmed. "Now think about how much I need to make a trade, and how much do I need to get to a quarter?"

After giving partners some time to think and talk, Kathy elicited their ideas, urging them to use the sentence frames for help. Following are examples of the responses from students:

- ✦ You need two more pennies.
- ✦ You need two more pennies to trade for a nickel.
- ✦ You need one more nickel to trade for a dime.
- ✦ You need seven more cents to trade for a quarter.
- ✦ You have eighteen cents, so you need two more pennies.

Kathy was pleased to garner a variety of ideas from volunteers. The sentence frames were flexible enough to accommodate a range of thinking, yet they provided enough structure to help students communicate their ideas.

Playing the Game

During the minilesson, Kathy had introduced the names and values of the coins, and she had explicitly taught the students how to use sentence frames to help them describe quantities of money and tell how to make trades.

When Kathy and Amanda were finished modeling the game, Kathy distributed to pairs of students one die; one zip-top sandwich bag of real coins, including thirty pennies, ten nickels, ten dimes, and one quarter; and one copy of the game rules.

Before dismissing them to their seats to play, Kathy established a rule: When a player is finished with his or her turn, the player must use at least one of the sentence frames before the other player can take a turn. This rule was intended to hold the students accountable for communicating their math thinking during the game. The frames were posted clearly on the board for all students to see (another idea is to distribute copies of the sentence frames for each pair of students to use while playing the game).

As Kathy circulated and observed students, she kept the following questions in mind:

- ✦ Which sentence frames are students using?
- ✦ Do students know when and how to make trades?

* Are students using the correct names and values for coins?
* How are students combining quantities when figuring the total for a mixed group of coins?
* How high can the English learners count in English?

Summarizing the Lesson

When everyone had a chance to finish at least one game of *Race for a Quarter*, Kathy directed the students to put away the money and dice and come to the rug.

Once the class was assembled, Kathy had the students review the names and values of the coins. She then read them a book called *A Quarter from the Tooth Fairy* (Holtzman 1995).

Before using this piece of literature with the students, Kathy had previewed the book for its appropriateness for English language learners. Although she knows that using literature in math class can provide interesting and familiar contexts for doing mathematics, Kathy is careful to make sure that the language in the book is accessible to ELLs. She evaluates a book for the sophistication of vocabulary, the complexity of the sentence structure, and the use of figurative language or idiomatic expressions. When using literature for the purpose of mathematics, Kathy wants to keep the focus on the mathematics and not have difficulties with the literature divert students' attention away from the math.

A Quarter from the Tooth Fairy is about a boy who starts out with a quarter he got from the tooth fairy. He buys a monster from his friend, but then changes his mind and returns it, getting his money back: two dimes and a nickel instead of a quarter. The boy in the story changes his mind over and over; each time he buys something, he returns it and gets back different coins that are worth twenty-five cents. Reading the story helped the children review the names and values of coins and how to trade for coins of equal value, and it was a perfect way to bring an end to the lesson.

Activity Directions ✦ **Trade Up for a Nickel**

1. Ask students what they know about money.

2. Show the students a penny and a nickel and ask them if they know the names and values of the coins.

3. Record the names and values of the coins on a vocabulary chart with corresponding pictures, and have students practice saying the names and values.

4. Show the students one of each amount card (1¢, 2¢, and 3¢). When showing each card, have students say the amount aloud and point to the picture of the coin on the vocabulary chart that equals the amount. Introduce the word *cents* and its symbol, and put it on the vocabulary chart.

5. Show the students the *Trade Up for a Nickel* game board. Model how to shuffle the amount cards, leaving them facedown in a pile after shuffling. Have a student volunteer choose a card, turn it over, and read the amount. Direct the class (or small group) to echo back the amount on the card. Have the student volunteer place that many pennies on the game board.

6. Ask the class, "How many pennies are there?" Check by counting the pennies along with the students, pointing to each penny as they count them. Then ask the students, "How many more pennies do we need in order to have five pennies?"

7. Introduce the sentence frames:

Beginning

> *I need _____ more _____ .*

Intermediate and Advanced

> *I have _____ , so I need _____ more _____ .*

> *I have _____ , so I can trade for _____ .*

Have students practice the frames, pausing for the blank spaces. Model using each of the frames, introducing the word *trade* when modeling the intermediate and advanced frames:

> *I have <u>three pennies</u> , so I need <u>two</u> more <u>pennies</u>.*

> *I have <u>five</u> pennies, so I can trade for <u>a nickel</u>.*

8. Continue modeling the game. Each time five pennies are filled up on the game board, make a trade for a nickel. When trading, point to the

word *trade*, say it aloud, and then have the students echo back. When you start to fill up the game board with pennies again, continue to ask the students these two questions:

- How many pennies are there?
- How many more pennies do we need to make a trade?

Have students use the sentence frames when responding to your questions.

9. Continue with the game until there are five nickels on the game board. With the students, count the number of nickels and then count the nickels aloud with the students by fives to twenty-five.

10. To each student, hand out a zip-top bag containing ten pennies and five nickels and a *Trade Up for a Nickel* game board. Ask the students to hold up a penny and review what it's worth. Ask the students to hold up a nickel and review what it's worth.

11. Play a game of *Trade Up for a Nickel* with the whole class (or a small group), asking for volunteers to turn over the amount cards. Have the students use the sentence frames to tell how many pennies they have and how many more pennies they need to make a trade.

Extending the Lesson

- Have the students play the game in pairs.
- Use these directions to play *Trade Up for a Dime* (using the *Trade Up for a Dime* game board and amount cards in the Blackline Masters). In this version, each student needs five dimes and fifteen pennies. Instead of trading for a nickel when they get five pennies, students trade for a dime when they get ten pennies. Introduce the vocabulary word *dime*. When all ten dimes are collected, students count how many dimes they have altogether and then count by tens to one dollar.
- Play *Race for a Quarter* (see Blackline Master for rules). In this game, introduce the vocabulary words *penny*, *nickel*, *dime*, and *quarter* as well as *money*, *cents*, and *trade*. Use the same sentence frames used in *Trade Up for a Nickel*. After students have had time to play the game, read *A Quarter from the Tooth Fairy* to bring closure to the lesson.

Would You Rather . . . ? 5

A Data Analysis Lesson

Day 1 and Day 2: Grades K, 1, and 2

Overview

In this lesson, students gain experience describing and comparing sets of data on a class graph. In a minilesson the first day, students choose between two different things they'd rather do at school (e.g., play on the swings or play on the slide). Data are gathered on a graph and the students are introduced to vocabulary words and a sentence frame that will help them describe and compare the data.

On Day 2 of the lesson, students listen to the book *Would You Rather . . .* , by John Burningham (2003). This children's book provides interesting contexts for creating graphs. Students respond to questions from a two-page spread in the book and then use key vocabulary and sentence frames to help them describe and compare data sets on a graph that is created.

Math Goal: Gather and represent data using graphs; describe and compare sets of data

Language Goal: Describe and compare sets of data

Key Vocabulary: equal, fewer, least, more, most

Materials

+ several pieces of chart paper for class graphs
+ sticky notes, 1 per student

- word cards for *more, fewer, most, least,* and *equal*
- pocket chart
- 2 sentence strips for sentence frames
- optional: *Would You Rather . . . ,* by John Burningham (2003)

Sentence Frames That Help Students Describe and Compare Sets of Data

Beginning

> *Beginning ELLs would be expected to use a one-word response.*

Intermediate and Advanced

> _____ *people would rather* _____ .

> _____ *people would rather* _____ *than* _____ .

Class Profile

In Cindy Green's class, all of her students are English language learners (ELLs). Of the twenty students in Cindy's class, ten are beginning English learners and the rest are in the intermediate and advanced range.

From the Classroom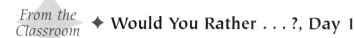

✦ Would You Rather . . . ?, Day 1

Minilesson Introducing Academic Language

Christine Sphar greeted the students in Cindy Green's class, who were assembled on the rug in the front of the room. Nineteen students were in class that day.

"Today we're going to talk about what we like to do," Christine told them. "Raise your hand if you have something that you like to do." Lots of hands shot into the air.

"Let's think about things you like to do at school," Christine said. "What do you like to do more, play on the slide or play on the swings?" To make sure that students knew what the words *slide* and *swing* meant, Christine pointed to a two-column chart she'd made, with pictures of a slide and a swing, accompanied by the words, at the top. As she said the words, Christine pointed to the pictures.

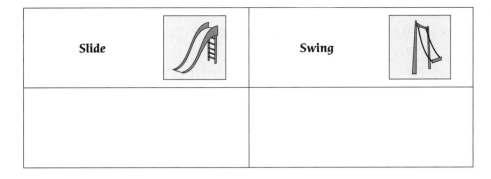

Slide		Swing	

"Point to where the *real* slide is at our school," Christine directed, helping students connect the pictures on the chart to the real world, thus allowing for greater comprehension. "Now point to where the *real* swing is at school."

"Would you rather play on the swings or play on the slide?" Christine asked again, rephrasing her question a bit. After waiting about five seconds to give students some time to decide, Christine elicited preferences from students.

"Ariana, would you rather play on the slide or play on the swings?" Christine asked.

"Play on slide," Ariana responded.

"I would rather . . . ," Christine prompted, pushing for more language.

"I would rather play on the slide," Ariana said.

"Let's all say that together," Christine told the class.

"I would rather play on the slide!" students chorused. Choral response is an effective way for students to practice expressive language.

Christine wrote Ariana's name on a sticky note and affixed it to the two-column chart under the picture of the slide. Christine continued to call on students one at a time, asking them what they would rather do and then writing their names on sticky notes and placing the notes on the chart.

Abby went next and gave a single-word response: "Swing."

Christine knows that Abby is a student with very beginning English language skills. She accepts different kinds of responses from students based on their level of English proficiency.

Isaiah, a student with intermediate-level fluency in English, responded, "I would rather play on the swings because it's fun." Isaiah demonstrated a higher level of English proficiency by adding his rationale without any prompting.

Continuing, Christine asked Karly, a student with stronger beginning English skills than Abby, "Would you rather play on the slide or play on the swing?" Christine was being consistent with this question, modeling the language structure she was looking for.

"Swing," Karly replied.

Instead of just accepting a single-word response as she did with Abby, Christine decided to provide some support to help Karly practice using more language. She did this by chunking out one part of the sentence at a time for Karly to repeat.

"I would rather . . . ," Christine modeled.

"I would rather," Karly said, copying Christine's example.

"Play on . . ."

"Play on," Karly responded.

"The swings . . ."

"The swings," Karly repeated, finishing up.

"I would rather play on the swings," Christine finally said, modeling the entire sentence.

When all the students had a chance to respond to Christine's question, the graph looked like this:

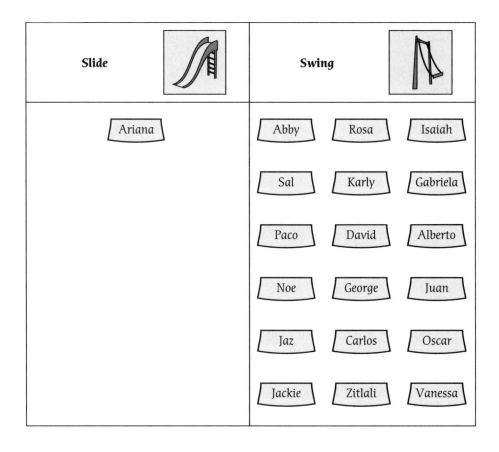

Next, Christine introduced the words *more* and *fewer* to the class. She did this by placing the two word cards in a pocket chart. Christine had the students say the words aloud and then held up two boxes of crayons; one box had more crayons than the other. Using realia, or real objects from the environment, can help bring meaning to words and concepts for English learners.

"This box has *more* crayons, and this box has *fewer* crayons," Christine said. As she always does when modeling language, Christine had the class repeat the sentence. She then introduced the first sentence frame by inserting it in the pocket chart:

_____ *people would rather* _____ .

Christine had the class practice saying the frame aloud, pausing for the blank spaces. She then said, "Let's take a look at our graph. Can someone use the sentence frame and the word *more* or *fewer* to describe our graph?"

"More people would rather play on the swings," Paco offered. Christine had the class repeat Paco's sentence in a choral voice, after inserting the word *more* into the frame:

More people would rather _____.

"Fewer people would rather play on the slide," Vanessa added. Christine inserted the word *fewer* in the frame. Once again, Christine had the students repeat the sentence, providing another structured opportunity for guided practice.

Fewer people would rather _____.

"How many people would rather play on the slide?" Christine asked the class.

"One!" the students responded.

"How can we find out how many people would rather play on the swings?" Christine queried.

"There's six in the first . . . ," Alberto began. He hesitated, not able to find a word for *column*.

"Come up and show us," Christine said. Having students show rather than tell is a helpful strategy for beginning and intermediate English language learners.

Alberto came up and pointed to the six sticky notes in the first column.

"So there's six in this *column*," Christine said, introducing this technical word with a light touch.

"There's six here and six here, that's twelve," Alberto continued, pointing to the first two columns of sticky notes. "And another six is . . ."

Christine helped out by directing the class to count on the remaining six sticky notes. The students counted, "Twelve, thirteen, fourteen . . ." all the way to eighteen.

"So it's six plus six plus six," Alberto summed up. Christine recorded the equation on the graph, thereby connecting Alberto's words with symbols.

$$6 + 6 + 6 = 18$$

"Is there another way we could figure out how many people would rather play on the swings?" Christine asked, looking for another strategy.

"Count by twos!" George suggested.

"If we count by twos, will we get the same answer as Alberto? Will there be eighteen?" Christine probed.

The idea that the amount does not change regardless of how one counts is an important idea that young children often do not understand. Christine had students put a thumb up if they thought that counting by twos would yield an answer of eighteen and thumb down if they didn't think so. Most students thought the answer would be the same. To check, Christine pointed to pairs of sticky notes as the class counted aloud by twos.

"Is there another way to check how many?" Christine asked the class.

"Count by fives!" Jaz exclaimed. Jaz walked up to the graph and said, "Cover up the ones at the bottom and count by fives, then count the ones you took off" (see illustration on facing page).

As Christine covered up the bottom three sticky notes, the class counted the rest by fives to get fifteen. Then Christine uncovered the three notes and the students counted on from fifteen to eighteen by ones.

"So no matter how we count them, we still get a total of eighteen," Christine summed up. "Could we use the number eighteen in this sentence frame?"

_____ *people would rather* _____.

"Eighteen people would rather play on the swings," Oscar offered. Christine led the students as they echoed Oscar's idea.

"Can anyone use a number to talk about the slide?" Christine asked.

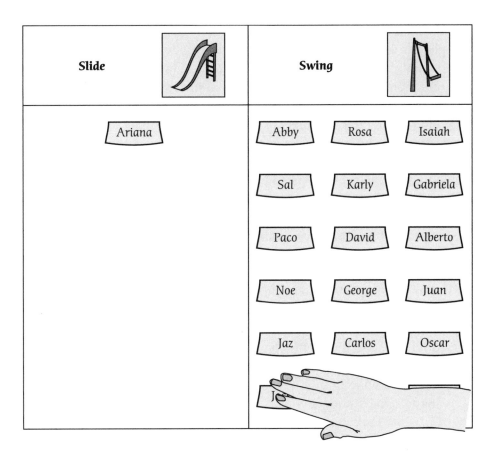

Slide		Swing		
Ariana		Abby	Rosa	Isaiah
		Sal	Karly	Gabriela
		Paco	David	Alberto
		Noe	George	Juan
		Jaz	Carlos	Oscar
		J...		

"One people would rather slide," responded Rosa.

"One person would rather play on the slide," Christine repeated, modeling correct use of grammar.

To finish the lesson for the day, Christine modeled another way to use the sentence frame to compare the quantities on the graph by saying, "Seventeen *more* people would rather swing than slide."

In the minilesson, Christine had introduced the children to an oral prompt (*Would you rather . . .*), a sentence frame (_____ *people would rather* _____), and key vocabulary words such as *more* and *fewer*. She had also provided students with opportunities to gather data about themselves, represent the data on a graph, and use language to describe and compare sets of data.

✦ Would You Rather . . . ?, Day 2

To begin Day 2 of the lesson, Christine asked the students what they remembered learning the previous day; all twenty students were in class that day. She pointed to the graph about swings and slides that they had completed. Tapping prior experiences helps students connect new learning to what they already know. This strategy allows for greater access to and retention of content and is especially important for English learners when the vocabulary associated with the content is unfamiliar.

After having the students talk with a partner, Christine regained students' attention by counting down from three, and then she called on David.

"How many likes swing and how many likes slide," he reported. David used the word *likes* instead of *would rather* to express his thought. This was fine with Christine because the sentence frames are there for support, not to inhibit students from using language they already know.

"So we found out how many people in the class would rather swing and how many would rather slide," Christine paraphrased, modeling correct use of grammar.

"More swing," Karly, a beginning English learner, offered. Christine was impressed that Karly used the new vocabulary word *more*; this signaled that her learning had transferred from the previous day and she could now use the word *more* to compare quantities.

Building on Karly's comment, Christine prompted, "More people would rather swing than . . ."

"Slide!" the students chorused.

Christine took this opportunity to introduce a new sentence frame. She had the class practice reading it aloud, pausing for the blank spaces.

> _____ people would rather _____ than _____.

She then took the time to explicitly teach the difference between *then* and *than*—two words that are similar and easily confused, even for native English speakers. Christine knows that when teaching English learners during math time, she is also teaching English, not just teaching *in* English.

Christine wrote the words *then* and *than* on the board and asked the students what letters were the same and different. She noted that the words almost sound the same, and had the students say the words aloud.

"The word *than* means the same as *instead*," Christine told the class. She then gave an example. "He would rather swing *instead* of slide. He would rather swing *than* slide."

After having the students review how to use the sentence frames to compare the data sets on the swing vs. slide graph, Christine introduced the children's book *Would You Rather . . .* , by John Burningham (2003). Before using this piece of literature with the students, Christine had previewed the book for its appropriateness for English language learners.

Although she knows that using literature in math class can provide interesting and familiar contexts for doing mathematics, Christine is careful to make sure that the language in the book is accessible to ELLs. She evaluates a book for the sophistication of vocabulary, the complexity of the sentence structure, and the use of figurative language or idiomatic expressions. When using literature for the purpose of mathematics, Christine wants to keep the focus on the mathematics and not have difficulties with the literature divert students' attention away from the math.

In the book *Would You Rather . . . ,* there are several pages that Christine found suitable to use as contexts for creating graphs as well as some pages that would be linguistically too complicated. Using the book isn't necessary for this lesson; teachers or students can make up their own questions and choices for graphs (e.g., Would you rather eat pizza, tacos, or hamburgers?). However, *Would You Rather . . .* is a book that children love. It's funny, engaging, and full of lively language and attention-grabbing illustrations.

Christine read the first two-page spread to the children, "Would you rather your house were surrounded by water, snow, or jungle?" After reading, Christine asked the students to give a simple show of hands. Next Christine introduced the word cards *most* and *least* and slipped them into the pocket chart next to the words *more* and *fewer.*

"Which one did people choose the *most*?" Christine asked.

"Jungle!" the students answered back. Indeed, most students had chosen jungle.

Christine pointed to the sentence frame and modeled for the class, "Most people would rather their house be surrounded by jungle." This sentence is a very difficult one for English learners and native speakers to produce. Therefore, Christine chose not to use this two-page spread as a context for creating a graph with the class.

"Which one did people choose the *least*?" Christine asked the class, pointing to the word *least* in the pocket chart.

"Water!"

Christine then continued to read the book until she got to the two-page spread that reads, "Would you rather be chased by a crab, a bull, a lion, or wolves?" She showed the students a piece of chart paper with this question written on it (see illustration on next page).

"What would you rather be chased by?" Christine asked the class. "Talk with a partner and share your idea." After a few seconds, she regained students' attention and began eliciting their choices.

"Which one would you rather be chased by, Carlos?" Christine asked.

"A lion!" Carlos exclaimed.

Would you rather be chased by...			
A Crab	**A Bull**	**A Lion**	**Wolves**

"I would rather be chased by . . . ," Christine prompted.

"I would rather be chased by a lion," Carlos responded.

Christine took the sticky note with Carlos's name from the slide vs. swing graph and affixed it in the Lion column.

"How about you, Rosa?" Christine queried.

"I would rather be chased by a crab because crabs are slow!" Rosa exclaimed. Rosa is a student with intermediate fluency in English. She correctly used the prompt that Christine modeled and provided a reason for her choice. Christine placed Rosa's sticky note on the graph underneath the heading "A Crab." She continued this process until she had collected half of the students' choices. The graph looked like this:

Would you rather be chased by...			
A Crab	**A Bull**	**A Lion**	**Wolves**
Rosa	Alberto	Carlos	Oscar
Abby		George	Zitlali
Karly		Jaz	
Paco			

"So far, which one has the *most*?" Christine asked the class, emphasizing the word *most*.

"Crab!" students replied.

"Let's use the sentence frame," Christine said, pointing to the frame in the pocket chart and inserting the word card *most* into the frame.

Most people would rather _____.

She modeled saying it first and then had the students echo back, "Most people would rather be chased by a crab."

"And which one has the *least*?" Christine pressed.

"Bull!" students exclaimed.

"Can someone use the other sentence frame?" Christine asked.

Using the frame for support, Isaiah said, "More people would rather be chased by a crab than a bull."

Catching on, Sal said, "More people would rather be chased by a crab than a lion."

"How many people would rather be chased by a crab?" Christine asked.

"Four!" the class shot back.

"A bull?" Christine continued.

"One!" the students chorused.

"A lion?"

"Three!"

"And chased by wolves?"

"Two!"

"*How many more* people would rather be chased by a crab than a lion?" Christine asked. Because *how many more* is typically a tricky question for children, Christine gave them several seconds to think and then called on Carlos.

"One," Carlos said.

"Why?" Christine asked, pushing for an explanation.

"There's four for crab and three for lion, so there's one more for crab," he explained.

When Carlos was finished, Gabriela walked up to the graph and removed one of the sticky notes from under the Crab column.

"I take one off and the crab and the lion are the same—three each," she explained. "And I put one back for the crab and that's one more."

"So you took one off the Crab column so that the number of sticky notes for the crab and the lion are equal," Christine paraphrased, modeling correct mathematical language. "And then you had one left over, and that told you that one more person would rather be chased by a crab than a lion." Carlos and Gabriela nodded in agreement.

Rosa went next. "I know that four take away three is one, so there's one more crab than lion," she reasoned.

Christine is always fishing for more and more mathematical explanations from the class, and will always give the students time to try to make sense of the math in their own way. When students are solving problems and communicating about their solution strategies, Christine finds that some students need more linguistic support, while others require more help with the math.

Christine continued to elicit students' choices until all of them had responded. The graph now looked like this:

Would you rather be chased by...			
A Crab	**A Bull**	**A Lion**	**Wolves**
Rosa	Alberto	Carlos	Oscar
Abby	Sal	George	Zitlali
Karly		Jaz	Noe
Paco		Gabriela	Juan
Vanessa		David	Jackie
Isaiah			
Juan			
Paul			

"Who can use one of the sentence frames to make a statement about the graph?" Christine asked the class.

"Most people would rather be chased by a crab," Isaiah reported. Isaiah is a student with advanced fluency and tends to be a strong model for his peers. Christine had the class repeat Isaiah's statement.

"Who can use some numbers in the sentence frame?" Christine asked.

"Eight people would rather be chased by a crab," Gabriela said.

"Five people would rather be chased by wolves," David added.

"Who can use the other sentence frame to talk about the graph?" Christine asked.

"More people would rather . . . ," Noe began and then fell silent.

Christine helped by prompting, "More people would rather be chased by . . ."

"More people would rather be chased by a crab than a bull," Noe said.

"What about these two?" Christine challenged, pointing to the columns for Lion and Wolves.

"They're the same!"

"What's another word for 'same amount'?" Christine asked the class.

"Equal!" several students replied.

Christine slipped the word card *equal* into the pocket chart and then, pointing at the column under the heading "A Lion," prompted, "Five people would rather be chased by . . ."

"A lion!" the class responded.

Purposely providing less support, Christine pointed at the column under the heading "Wolves" and prompted, "Five people . . ."

"Would rather be chased by wolves!"

"So they are *equal,* or the *same amount,*" Christine summed up, recasting the math term to help the students understand.

Christine brought an end to the lesson by having the students figure out the total number of sticky notes on the graph. She told the students that they would be using the children's book later in the week to create more graphs for math class.

Extensions

+ Read a different two-page spread each day to create different questions and choices for graphs.
+ After reading a two-page spread in the book, have the students create a human graph. For example, all the students who would rather be lost in the fog stand in a group; all the students who would rather be lost at sea stand in a group; all the students who would rather be lost in the desert form a group; and so on.

✦ Have the students come up with their own questions for a graph. Then direct the students to collect, organize, and analyze the data on their own or with a partner.

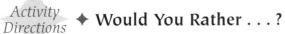

Activity Directions ✦ **Would You Rather . . . ?**

Day 1

Minilesson Introducing Academic Language

1. Ask students a question that can be answered and represented on a graph. The question should be something with which the children are familiar. For example, you might ask, "Which do you like to do more, play on the swings or play on the slide?" Rephrase this question, asking, "Would you rather play on the swings or play on the slide?"

2. Show the class a two-column chart, labeled with the words *Swing* and *Slide* at the top. The words should have pictures accompanying them.

3. Ask the question again ("Would you rather play on the swings or play on the slide?"), and have students raise their hands to indicate their preferences. As students report their choices, write each of their names on a sticky note and place the notes on the graph.

4. When all the sticky notes have been affixed to the graph, ask the students what they notice about the graph. Introduce the vocabulary words *more* and *less*.

5. Ask the students, "Which do people like more, playing on the swings or playing on the slide?" Rephrase this question by asking, "Which would people rather do more, play on the swings or the slide?"

   ELLs at a beginning level might answer with a one-word response. Introduce the following sentence frame, appropriate for intermediate and advanced ELLs:

> _____ *people would rather* _____ .

6. Elicit responses from students, encouraging them to use the sentence frame for support.

7. Rearrange the sticky notes, this time creating a bar graph so that students can more easily see how many more responses one category got than another or see if they received an equal number.

8. Ask the students to compare the data sets with the question, "How many more people would rather _____ than _____?" Beginning-level ELLs might use a one-word response, while intermediate and advanced ELLs can use the sentence frame (e.g., "Three more people would rather swing than slide.").

Day 2

Creating More Graphs

Take a few minutes to create your own questions for graphing. Or, as an alternative, read the book *Would You Rather . . .* to the class. As you read, clarify new or difficult words for the students. Choose a few pages as questions for graphs. For each page or two-page spread, follow these steps:

1. Ask the question from the book.
2. Write the choices on chart paper to create a graph.
3. Elicit responses from the students and record their responses on the graph.
4. Ask the students:
   ✦ What do you notice?
   ✦ Which do people like more, _____ or _____?
   ✦ How many more people would rather _____ than _____?

Encourage students to use the sentence frames for support when responding. Introduce the words *most, least,* and *equal* to help students expand their responses.

6 Cubes in a Tube

An Algebra Lesson

GRADE-LEVEL RECOMMENDATIONS

Day 1: Grades K, 1, and 2
Day 2: Grades 1 and 2

Overview

In this activity, students gain experience with identifying, describing, and extending repeating patterns. They do this by predicting the color pattern of a cube train that is hidden inside a roll of newsprint, creating their own cube train, and reproducing the train's repeating color pattern on a 1–100 chart.

In a minilesson before working with the cube trains, students are introduced to vocabulary words and sentence frames that will help them describe patterns and use patterns to make predictions.

Math Goal: Identify, describe, extend, and make predictions about patterns

Language Goal: Describe and make predictions

Key Vocabulary: action, cube, diagonal, horizontal, pattern, predict, prediction, repeating, vertical, and words to describe the colors of the cubes used (e.g., red, blue, green, yellow, white, brown, etc.)

Materials

✦ vocabulary word cards for *pattern, repeating, predict, action, prediction, cube, vertical, horizontal, diagonal,* and names of cube colors
✦ pocket chart
✦ 3 sentence strips for sentence frames
✦ interlocking cubes, 20 per student and 20 for each cube train the teacher will present
✦ 1 sheet of 18-inch newsprint for each cube train the teacher will present

- small sticky notes, 1 per student
- 1–100 charts, 1 per student and 1 to use when modeling for the class (see Blackline Masters)
- crayons to match color pattern in cube trains used for modeling
- boxes of crayons, 1 per student

Sentence Frames That Help Students Make Predictions

Beginning

> Beginning ELLs would be expected to use a one-word response for the color of the cube.

Intermediate and Advanced

> I predict the next _____ will be _____.

> I predict the next _____ will be _____ because _____.

Sentence Frames That Help Students Describe Patterns

Beginning

> Beginning ELLs would be expected to state the colors in the pattern.

Intermediate and Advanced

> The pattern is _____.

Class Profile

Of the twenty students in Sharon Fargason's class, all but one student is an English language learner (ELL). Two students are beginning English speakers, eight have intermediate fluency, nine are advanced English speakers, and one student is a native English speaker.

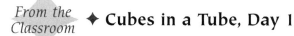

From the Classroom ◆ **Cubes in a Tube, Day 1**

Minilesson Introducing Academic Language

Kathy Melanese greeted the students in Sharon Fargason's class and immediately began a pattern by taking her hands and slapping them against her lap, and then clapping her hands together; she kept up this cyclical repetition, directing the students to join her in the slap-clap-slap-clap pattern. The students in the class enthusiastically complied.

At a certain point, Kathy stopped participating, but the students kept slapping and clapping, repeating the pattern they had learned.

"Wow!" Kathy exclaimed. "You all knew what to do even after I stopped slapping and clapping! How did you do that?"

"'Cause it keeps going over and over," Daisy said.

"It's like a circle, it keeps going and going," Vi explained. Daisy and Vi are both students with advanced fluency in English; Vi's native language is Vietnamese and Daisy's first language is Spanish.

"We made a *pattern*," Kathy told the class, emphasizing the new word and placing a card in the pocket chart with the word *pattern* written on it. She read the word aloud and then had the students echo back.

"Let's try again," Kathy said. She began the slap-clap-slap-clap pattern again and the students followed along. When she stopped, she addressed the class.

"Our pattern *repeats*," she said, "It goes over and over."

Kathy then introduced a sentence frame, fitting it in the pocket chart on the board.

```
┌─────────────────────────────────────────┐
│                                           │
│   ┌──────────┐                            │
│   │ pattern  │ _____     │
│   └──────────┘                            │
│   _____        │
│                                           │
│   _____        │
│                                           │
│   _____        │
│                                           │
│   ┌──────────────────────────────┐        │
│   │ The pattern is _____ .  │        │
│   └──────────────────────────────┘        │
│   _____        │
│                                           │
│   _____        │
│                                           │
│   _____        │
│                                           │
│   _____        │
│                                           │
└─────────────────────────────────────────┘
```

She read it aloud to the students, pausing for the blank space. Kathy then inserted in the frame a card with the word *repeating* written on it:

```
┌─────────────────────────────────────────┐
│                                           │
│   ┌──────────┐                            │
│   │ pattern  │ _____     │
│   └──────────┘                            │
│   _____        │
│                                           │
│   _____        │
│                                           │
│   _____        │
│                                           │
│   ┌──────────────────────────────────┐    │
│   │ The pattern is │repeating│ .     │    │
│   └──────────────────────────────────┘    │
│   _____        │
│                                           │
│   _____        │
│                                           │
│   _____        │
│                                           │
└─────────────────────────────────────────┘
```

After Kathy read the frame, she had the students echo it back several times. Then she described the pattern in another way, using the same sentence frame.

"The pattern is slap-clap-slap-clap-slap-clap," she said to the class. Again, Kathy had the students repeat after her as she pointed to the words in the sentence frame.

Next, Kathy placed the word card *predict* in the pocket chart. After she read the word aloud and had the students say it several times, she tapped students' prior knowledge by asking them what they thought the word meant. She gave them some think time to formulate their ideas; this is a strategy that is helpful to all students, but crucial for English language learners.

When several seconds had passed, Kathy called on Oscar. Although Oscar is an intermediate-level English speaker, he has strong math skills. Kathy is careful not to make assumptions about a student's math ability based on his linguistic expertise in English.

"To predict something, you read a book and you sometimes predict something," Oscar explained.

"Does anyone have anything to add to what Oscar said?" Kathy asked the class.

"When a teacher reads a book, what's going to happen . . . you predict what's going to happen next," Ayomide offered.

"Oscar and Ayomide made a good connection," Kathy observed. "We can make predictions, or predict, when we read. We also make predictions when we do science and when we do math."

She then said, "I'm going to do another slap-clap pattern, but this time it's going to be different. I'm going to make the pattern and I want you to watch and listen. When I stop, I want you to turn to a partner and *predict* or guess what *action* comes next." Kathy often uses familiar words, like *guess*, along with new academic vocabulary to make content more comprehensible to English learners. Before starting her next pattern, Kathy placed a card with the word *action* written on it in the pocket chart and repeated her direction (see illustration on facing page).

"Are you ready?" she began. "Remember, when I stop, I want you to turn to your partner and predict what *action* will come next. The action will be a slap or a clap." She then had the students practice saying the word *action* aloud in a choral voice.

Kathy's new repeating pattern went like this: slap-clap-clap-slap-clap-clap, and so on. After repeating the pattern several times so that students could recognize the identifiable unit that repeated (slap-clap-clap), Kathy stopped after a slap. She then directed the students to turn

```
┌─────────────────────────────────────────────┐
│                                               │
│   [pattern]              [predict]            │
│   ───────────────────────────────────────     │
│   [action]                                    │
│   ───────────────────────────────────────     │
│                                               │
│   ───────────────────────────────────────     │
│                                               │
│   ───────────────────────────────────────     │
│                                               │
│                                               │
│   The pattern is [repeating].                 │
│   ───────────────────────────────────────     │
│                                               │
│   ───────────────────────────────────────     │
│                                               │
│   ───────────────────────────────────────     │
│                                               │
│   ───────────────────────────────────────     │
│                                               │
└─────────────────────────────────────────────┘
```

to a partner and predict what would come next. The students were excited; they could hardly contain themselves.

"It's clap-clap!" several students shouted. Kathy had to remind them to use quiet voices and to raise their hands. So that everyone could participate, Kathy let the students show what action would happen next. Relieved, the students clapped twice. Then Kathy placed a new sentence frame in the pocket chart, designed to help students make predictions.

> *I predict the next* _____ *will be* _____.

"So everyone thought that clap-clap would come next," Kathy reminded. "We can say that in a complete sentence." She then had the students practice their prediction using the sentence frame. First she modeled, and then she had the class echo back.

"I predict the next action will be clap-clap!"

Kathy presented one more pattern to the class that went like this: slap-slap-slap-clap-clap-slap-slap-slap-clap-clap, and so on. Once again, Kathy slapped and clapped just enough for the students to be able to recognize how the pattern worked; she then stopped after three slaps. With enthusiasm, most of the students clapped two times to extend the pattern.

"Who can tell us what your prediction is for the action that will come next?" Kathy asked the class. After waiting for many hands to be raised, she called on Vi.

"What's your prediction, Vi?" Kathy asked.

Vi's response was to clap two times. Kathy pushed for the use of language by pointing to the sentence frame and encouraging Vi to use it to help her make a prediction.

With a little guidance from Kathy and looking up at the frame, Vi said, "I predict that the next action will be . . ."

Vi stalled. To help out, Kathy clapped two times and asked, "What's this called?"

"Clap," Vi responded. "I predict the next action will be clap."

"Thumbs up if you agree with Vi, and thumbs down if you disagree," Kathy directed. She wanted to give everyone an opportunity to respond nonverbally, especially the students with beginning skills in English.

Before moving on, Kathy repeated the pattern once again, but this time she stopped after clap-clap. Many of the students continued the pattern by slapping three times.

"How did you know that the next action would be three slaps?" Kathy asked the class. As she posed this question, Kathy placed a new sentence frame in the pocket chart. This frame was slightly different than the other frame for predicting.

I predict the next _____ will be _____ because _____.

Kathy prompted the students by saying, "I predict that the next action will be slap-slap-slap because . . ."

"Because it will be . . . ," Buruj began and then stumbled.

Kathy prompted her again, repeating the sentence frame, "I predict the next action will be slap-slap-slap because . . ."

"Because I knew it was a slap because I used the clap and clap and then the slap-slap-slap comes next," Buruj explained.

Sarah, an advanced English speaker, exclaimed, "I knew it because it is a pattern!"

Building on Sarah's comment, Kathy modeled using the sentence frame. "I predict the next action will be slap-slap-slap because it is a pattern." She then had the class echo back several times for practice.

Ayomide went next, reporting, "I predict the next will be a slap-slap-slap because the pattern repeats." Kathy was pleased that Ayomide used a key vocabulary word (*repeats*) to explain her thinking.

Using the sentence frame for support, Ashely said, "I predict the next action will be a slap-slap-slap because I know the pattern goes slap-slap-slap-clap-clap-slap-slap-slap."

Kathy brought an end to the minilesson by telling the students that they would be exploring more repeating patterns in a minute, using different-colored cubes. To make sure that students knew the names of the colors, Kathy showed them one colored cube at a time, directing the class to say the name aloud. Each time Kathy showed a colored cube, she placed a word card on the board with the color word written on it along with a corresponding colored dot. The students were familiar with most of the color names; only a few stumbled on the colors *yellow* and *brown*. Kathy made a mental note of this, so she could pay particular attention to those students during the upcoming lesson on patterns.

Introducing the Activity

To begin the lesson, Kathy held up a tube made from a rolled-up piece of newsprint, 18 inches in length, for the students to see. Hidden inside the paper tube was a train of twenty interlocking cubes that were arranged in a repeating *ab* pattern:

"Wow! That's a big sword!" Micky exclaimed. The students giggled.

"Inside this paper tube are cubes snapped together to make a train," Kathy explained. "What color do you think the first cube will be?"

The students offered a variety of predictions: green, blue, red, and so on. When they were finished guessing, Kathy slowly revealed the first cube, which was white. The students were excited.

"What do you think the color of the next cube will be? What's your *prediction*?" Kathy asked the class, exaggerating her tone when saying *prediction* and pointing to the word in the pocket chart. In one of the sentence frames, she inserted a card with the word *cube* written on it:

> *I predict the next <u>cube</u> will be _____.*

Kathy had the students practice the sentence frame, pausing for the blank space, and then had them turn to a partner and share their predictions. Some thought the next cube would be brown, others predicted white, still others guessed different colors. When the students finished making predictions, Kathy ever so slowly revealed the second cube, which was brown. She had everyone say the color aloud, making sure that all of the students were participating.

"What do you predict the next cube will be?" Kathy asked. "Whisper your prediction to your neighbor."

After a couple of seconds, Kathy elicited some predictions from students.

"Green," Axel guessed. Kathy was pleased that Axel was participating. He is a recent immigrant and has beginning English skills.

"So you predict that the next cube will be green?" Kathy confirmed, modeling a complete sentence for Axel.

"I predict another white," Sarah said.

"Why?" Kathy pressed, pushing for an explanation. "You predict white because . . . ," she prompted.

"Because I think it's going to be a pattern," Sarah replied. "White-brown-white-brown."

"Let's practice Sarah's prediction," Kathy told the class. With Kathy leading, the students chorused, "I predict the next cube will be white because it's going to be a pattern."

"I think it's going to be white," Micky said.

"I predict . . . ," Kathy prompted.

"I predict the next cube will be white," Micky said, extending his language.

Kathy slid another cube from the tube, revealing a white one. The students became animated.

"I knew it!"

"It's a pattern!"

Kathy continued to reveal one cube at a time until the entire train was exposed. Along with the students, Kathy "read" the pattern: "White-brown-white-brown, . . . ," all the way to the twentieth cube, which was brown.

Next, Kathy held up the cube train for the class to see and told the students to talk with a partner about the pattern. After several seconds, she regained their attention and elicited descriptions.

"It's a pattern!" Gurkan exclaimed excitedly.

"The pattern is *ababab*!" Oscar shouted. Kathy was impressed by Oscar's ability to recognize the pattern and use letters to symbolize it. He was obviously tapping into his prior knowledge and experience.

"It's white-brown-white-brown," Ana added.

"The pattern is . . . ," Kathy prompted, pointing to the sentence frame.

The students answered, "The pattern is white-brown-white-brown-white-brown."

"We can also say that the pattern is repeating; it's going over and over: white-brown-white-brown," Kathy noted. She then had the students echo back.

"What if we were clapping and slapping—what would the pattern look and sound like?" Kathy asked. As she pointed to each cube, the students began a clap-slap pattern. Identifying the same pattern in different forms (e.g., with cubes and with clapping and slapping) and using patterns to make predictions should be an important part of children's early experiences with patterns.

Next, Kathy showed the class another cube train that was hidden inside a tube. Unlike the *ab* pattern she showed before, this time she had an *abc* pattern hidden inside: red-green-blue-red-green-blue, and so on. As before, she elicited predictions from students before revealing each cube. She pushed students to use the following sentence frames to discuss their predictions and to describe the pattern:

I predict the next cube will be _____.

I predict the next cube will be _____ *because* _____.

The pattern is _____.

Observing the Students

Kathy knows that it's important for students to be able to explore on their own and have firsthand experience with making patterns and talking about them. So when she was finished with *Cubes in a Tube* with the whole class, she gave students oral directions for making cube trains at their tables:

1. Make a cube train twenty cubes long; the cubes in the train must make a repeating pattern.
2. When you're finished with the cube train, describe the repeating pattern to your teacher and a neighbor.
3. Have your neighbor try to predict what color cube will come next in your train (that is, what color the twenty-first cube will be).

After dismissing the students, Kathy circulated. As she observed, she made sure that each student was following directions and using the sentence frames to describe her pattern and make predictions about her neighbor's pattern.

Kathy listened in as Felipe, a beginning English learner, described the pattern he'd made.

"Black-black," he said, pointing to the first two cubes in his train. He stopped as he touched the next cube, which was brown.

Kathy used Felipe's native language, Spanish, as a resource and said, "Café."

Touching the brown cube, Felipe repeated, "Café."

Kathy then touched the cube and said, "In English, it's *brown*."

Felipe repeated the color name in English and then continued describing his pattern to Kathy, "Black-black-brown-black-black-brown . . . ," all the way to the end of his cube train.

B B Br B B Br B B Br B B Br B B Br B B Br B B Br B B

When Felipe was finished describing his pattern, Kathy pointed to the color chart on the wall and reminded Felipe that he could use it as a resource if he forgot a color word.

Kathy turned to Felipe's neighbor, Leonardo, and asked him to predict what color cube would come next in Felipe's cube train, after the twentieth cube.

Leonardo read the colors aloud in the cube train and then said, "I think brown will come next."

"Use the sentence frame to help you," Kathy encouraged, pointing to one of the frames in the pocket chart.

With some help from Kathy, Leonardo said, "I predict that the next cube will be brown."

"Leonardo, what can you say about Felipe's pattern?" Kathy asked.

"It goes black-black-brown-black-black-brown," he replied, touching each cube as he spoke.

"The pattern goes over and over," Kathy said to him. "The pattern . . ."

Leonardo paused; the word just wasn't coming to him.

"Repeats," Kathy said. "The pattern repeats."

"The pattern repeats," Leonardo echoed.

When Kathy visited Ana's desk, she was helping Axel, a beginning English speaker, with the color word *yellow*.

"In Spanish, it's *amarillo*," she said to Axel. "In English, it's *yellow*."

Using bilingual students to translate for other students can be helpful, especially if the classroom teacher doesn't know the child's native language.

The students were very engaged as they built their cube trains. Depending on students' English language proficiency, the language they used to describe and predict varied. Some students used one-word responses to predict the color of the next cube in their neighbor's train, while other students used the sentence frames to produce complete sentences when talking about the patterns. Kathy's goal was to make sure everyone was able to use language to communicate about patterns.

A Class Discussion

When students were finished, Kathy asked them to leave their cube trains at their tables and come to the rug. Once they were assembled, she held up one of the student's trains for everyone to see.

"Let's read Gurkan's pattern," Kathy told the class.

As she pointed to each cube, the students chorused, "Blue-red-green-blue-red-green . . . ," all the way to the twentieth cube, which was red.

"Who can describe Gurkan's pattern for us in another way?" Kathy asked the class.

"The pattern is repeating," Tim said. "It goes over and over."

"The pattern is twenty cubes long," Sarah observed.

"The pattern is a three-color pattern; it has blue, red, green," Daniel commented.

"The twentieth cube is red," Kathy said, pointing to the last cube in Gurkan's cube train. "Turn to your neighbor and predict what color you think the twenty-first cube will be." After a few seconds, Kathy called on Tim to share his prediction.

"I predict that the next cube will be green," he said.

"Why?" Kathy probed.

As Kathy waited to give Tim some think time, she thought about how difficult it had been for many of the students to provide reasons for their predictions. To help students explain their thinking, Kathy planned to continue to model, prompt, and encourage students to use key vocabulary and the sentence frames.

When she thought Tim was ready, Kathy prompted, "You think the next cube will be green because . . ."

"Because I think about it," he said.

Ayomide chimed in, "Because I know it already."

"I predict that the next cube will be green because it repeats," Buruj added. Buruj is a student with advanced fluency, whose native language is Somali.

"So Buruj knows that the next cube will be green because the pattern repeats," Kathy summed up. She then touched one cube at a time on Gurkan's train and said, "The pattern goes over and over: blue-red-green-blue-red-green and so on. The pattern is predictable."

To end the lesson, Kathy collected the students' cube trains, placing them in a tub for the next day. To keep track of the trains, she put little sticky notes on them, each labeled with a student's name.

✦ Cubes in a Tube, Day 2

Extending Patterns on the 1–100 Chart

To begin math class, Kathy gathered the students on the rug and held up one of the cube trains she had hidden inside a paper tube the day before. The cubes in the train formed a repeating pattern: white-brown-white-brown, and so on. The students recognized the cube train and began commenting.

"It's a pattern!"

"It's a repeating pattern!"

"It goes white-brown-white-brown!"

Some students began to make a clap-slap repeating pattern with their hands to show a different way to represent the pattern. Kathy was pleased that the students remembered.

"Who can remind us about what we learned yesterday?" Kathy asked the class, always taking an opportunity to tap students' prior knowledge and give them a chance to talk in math class.

"We learned about patterns," Tim reminded everyone.

"We learned that patterns can repeat; they can go on and on and on," Sarah added.

"We predicted!" Oscar exclaimed, pointing to the sentence frames.

"Today, you're going to take the cube train you made yesterday and color the pattern on a one-to-one hundred chart," Kathy said, pointing to the chart she'd posted on the board. "If I'm going to use crayons to make the cube train pattern on this chart, which crayon colors will I need?"

"Brown!"

"White!"

"I'm just going to use the brown crayon for my pattern," Kathy explained. "I can leave the spaces blank that will be white."

Kathy modeled how to color in the 1–100 chart to show the repeating pattern on the cube train. She began by leaving the first square blank to represent white and then colored in the next square brown. Kathy continued coloring in squares on the chart, asking for the students' help as she went. Occasionally, Kathy had the students use the following sentence frame to make predictions about what color would come next on the chart:

> I predict that the next cube will be _____ because _____.

When she had finished coloring in the fiftieth square, the chart looked like this (see illustration on next page).

"Let's look at the pattern now," Kathy told the class. "What do you notice about the pattern on the one-to-one hundred chart? Talk to a partner about what you notice."

After a few seconds, Kathy elicited a few ideas from students.

"All the browns are odd," Ashley observed.

"All the browns are odd . . . ," Kathy prompted.

"All the browns are odd numbers," Ashley replied.

Kathy continued, "So all the whites are . . ."

"Even!" several students chorused.

The class had recently been learning about odds and evens, indicated by a chart on the wall that explained about these numbers. Kathy was pleased that the students had made this connection. If they hadn't, she would have helped them do so.

"What else do you notice?" Kathy asked.

Cubes in a Tube

1	2	3	4	5	6	7	8	9	10
11	12	13	14	15	16	17	18	19	20
21	22	23	24	25	26	27	28	29	30
31	32	33	34	35	36	37	38	39	40
41	42	43	44	45	46	47	48	49	50
51	52	53	54	55	56	57	58	59	60
61	62	63	64	65	66	67	68	69	70
71	72	73	74	75	76	77	78	79	80
81	82	83	84	85	86	87	88	89	90
91	92	93	94	95	96	97	98	99	100

"The pattern goes white-brown-white-brown," Jonathan said.

"The browns and whites go up and down," Dariana observed.

Kathy used this opportunity to introduce the word *vertical* to the class. She posted the word card in the pocket chart and had the class say it aloud. The word had an arrow drawn next to it to provide a visual clue:

In addition, Kathy gestured with her hands in an up-and-down motion, directing the students to do the same as they repeated the word *vertical* aloud. Gesturing gives English learners a visual clue for a word's meaning.

After introducing the word *vertical*, Kathy did the same for the words *horizontal* and *diagonal*, each time having the students gesture while saying the words aloud. She told the students that they would be coloring in patterns on their own charts, and that some of their patterns might create *vertical*, *horizontal*, and *diagonal* lines.

Because there were several students in Sharon's class whose native language is Spanish, Kathy briefly mentioned to the students that the words *vertical*, *horizontal*, and *diagonal* are cognates and are very similar to those words in Spanish: *vertical, horizontal,* and *diagonal.* Kathy is careful not to assume that the native Spanish speakers will automatically recognize these words in their native language. Students' awareness of academic language depends on their prior experience. Nevertheless, Kathy takes every opportunity in math class to bridge English with students' native languages.

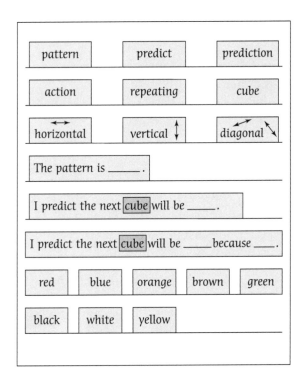

Pointing to the one hundredth square on the chart, Kathy asked, "Can you predict what color the one hundredth square will be? Will it be brown or white? Talk to a neighbor about your prediction." The chart was colored in up to the fiftieth square. Kathy wanted the students to use the pattern on the chart to make a prediction beyond the fiftieth square. After a few seconds, she called on Leonardo.

Using the sentence frames for support, Leonardo explained, "I predict the one hundred will be white because all the tens are white and you can just look down."

Kathy pointed to each of the numbers in the column Leonardo was referring to and had the students count by tens to one hundred. Starting from the fifty-first square, Kathy had the class chant the color pattern as she pointed to each of the remaining squares on the chart to verify Leonardo's prediction.

Cubes in a Tube

Kathy asked the students to predict the color of a few other squares on the 1–100 chart that were not yet colored in. When students were finished making predictions, she quickly colored in all of the remaining squares up to one hundred to complete the pattern and then gave the class directions for their next task:

1. Take your cube train back to your desk.
2. Color in the cube train pattern on your 1–100 chart.
3. Describe the cube train pattern to a neighbor.

Kathy distributed to each student her or his cube train and a chart and then dismissed them all to their seats to work on their patterns. As they worked, Kathy circulated, helping out when needed.

A Class Discussion

When the students were finished, Kathy transitioned them back to the rug, directing them to leave their cube trains and 1–100 charts at their tables. She asked a few students for permission to show their charts to the class in the upcoming discussion.

When the students were settled, Kathy held up Kenneth's pattern (see Figure 6–1.)

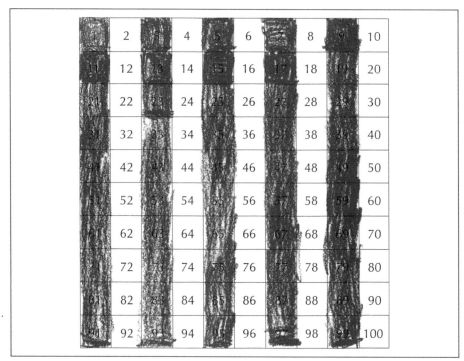

FIGURE 6-1. Kenneth's vertical pattern.

Kathy asked the students to describe Kenneth's pattern. Pointing to the sentence frame on the board, she prompted, "The pattern is . . ."

"The pattern is going on and on," Vi said. As Vi shared, Kathy wrote her words on the board.

"The pattern is red-white-red-white," Buruj added. Again, Kathy wrote the words on the board to model writing and to provide a word bank for students. She continued to record words as each student reported.

"The pattern is repeating!" Gracie exclaimed.

"The pattern has vertical lines," Kenneth chimed in.

"The odd numbers are red," Sarah observed.

Next, Kathy held up Tyler's 1–100 chart. His chart was colored in up to 30. (See Figure 6–2.)

"What do you notice about Tyler's pattern?" Kathy asked the class.

"The pattern has lines that go like this," Gurkan said, motioning a diagonal line with his hands.

Pointing to the word *diagonal* on the vocabulary chart, Kathy reminded Gurkan of the correct terminology and had him repeat his observation.

"All the colors go in diagonals," Dariana added. "The blacks, the greens, and yellows."

"So the pattern has black, green, and yellow diagonal lines," Kathy rephrased.

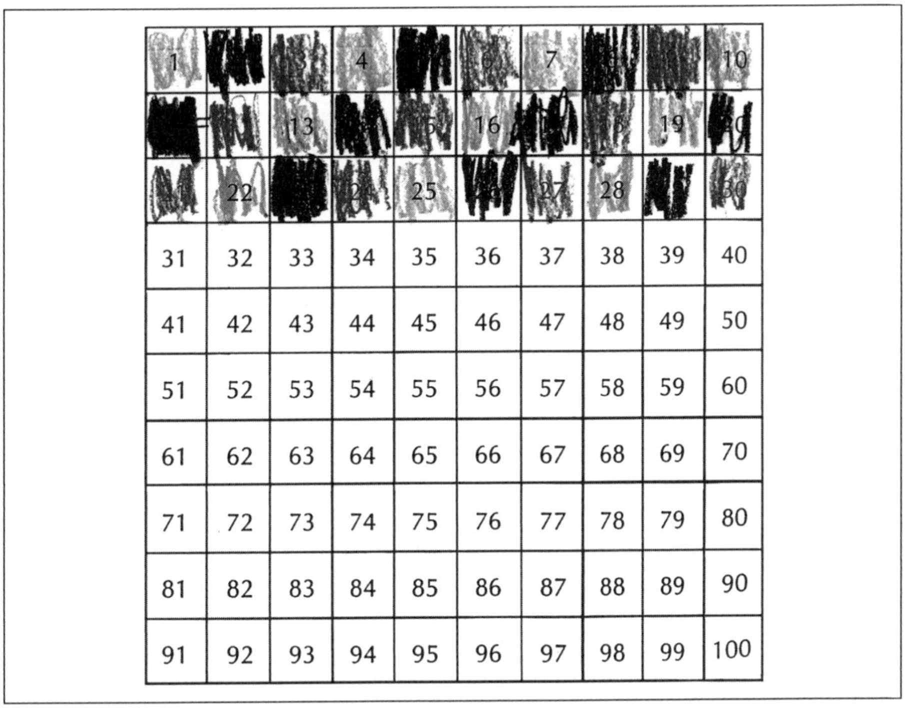

FIGURE 6–2. Tyler's diagonal pattern.

To help the students make predictions from the pattern, Kathy pointed to the thirty-fifth square on Tyler's chart and asked them what color they thought the thirty-fifth cube would be. She gave the students time to talk with a partner and then called on Gracie, a native English speaker. Kathy pointed to the sentence frame to get Gracie started.

"I predict it will be black," Gracie said. She came up and pointed to the right-to-left diagonal line that the eighth, seventeenth, and twenty-sixth squares made on the 1–100 chart.

"So Gracie predicts that the thirty-fifth cube will be black because of this diagonal line," Kathy paraphrased, pointing to the chart.

After asking the students to make a few more predictions about the colors of the squares on Tyler's chart, Kathy concluded the lesson by providing the students with another opportunity to describe their patterns, this time in writing. (See Figures 6–3 through 6–6.)

1	2	3	4	5	6	7	8	9	10
11	12	13	14	15	16	17	18	19	20
21	22	23	24	25	26	27	28	29	30
31	32	33	34	35	36	37	38	39	40
41	42	43	44	45	46	47	48	49	50
51	52	53	54	55	56	57	58	59	60
61	62	63	64	65	66	67	68	69	70
71	72	73	74	75	76	77	78	79	80
81	82	83	84	85	86	87	88	89	90
91	92	93	94	95	96	97	98	99	100

It is Vertical. The Even ones are yellow. It gos on and on.

FIGURE 6-3. Sarah used mathematical language to describe her pattern.

My pattern is ~~Dieagonl~~ Diagonal
It's ~~Colors~~ are orng blue,
yellow. They Repeat.

FIGURE 6-4.
Gracie
described her
pattern.

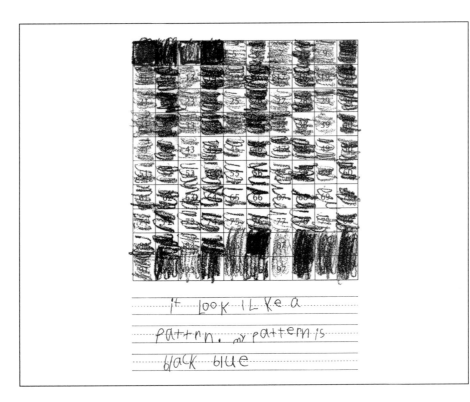

It look lLke a
PAttrn. my PAttern is
blaCK bLue

FIGURE 6-5.
This inter-
mediate-level
English
speaker used
a few words
to describe
his pattern.

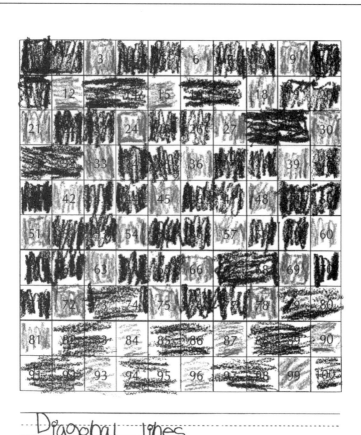

FIGURE 6-6. This beginning English speaker used a few words to describe his pattern.

Diagonal lines

Modifications for Younger Children

+ Because some younger children are not yet reading, use the sentence frames orally instead of having students read them. You can still post the sentence frames as a reminder to yourself of how to help support students.
+ Teach only Day 1 of *Cubes in a Tube*.
+ When teaching Day 2, rather than use a complete 1–100 chart on which to represent the repeating cube train pattern, give each student a chart with fewer squares (e.g., 1–20, 1–30, 1–40, or 1–50).

Day 1

Minilesson Introducing Academic Language

1. Model a slap-clap-slap-clap pattern and have the students join in.

2. Introduce the words *pattern* and *repeats* and *repeating* to the class.

3. Introduce the following sentence frame:

> *The pattern is _____.*

Have the students practice using the sentence frame with the word *repeating*.

4. Introduce the words *predict* and *prediction*.

5. Introduce the word *action* to the class. Model a new pattern: slap-clap-clap-slap-clap-clap. Have the students predict what the next action will be in the pattern. Introduce the following sentence frames to help students make their predictions:

> *I predict the next _____ will be _____.*

> *I predict the next _____ will be _____ because _____.*

6. Hold up one colored cube and its corresponding color word card at a time for the students to see. Direct the students to practice saying the color words aloud.

Introducing the Activity

1. Using twenty interlocking cubes, make a cube train that has a repeating *ab* pattern.

2. Make a tube just long enough to hide the cube train by rolling up a piece of 18-inch newsprint and taping it together so that it doesn't unroll. Hide the cube train inside.

3. Show the tube with the train hidden inside to the students. Ask them to predict what color the first cube will be and have them share their predictions, using the sentence frames for support.

4. After students share their predictions, reveal the color of the first cube.

5. Repeat Step 4 for each cube in the train until you have removed the entire train from the tube.

6. Show the students the cube train and have them make observations about the pattern, using the sentence frames for support.

7. Distribute interlocking cubes so that each student has enough cubes to make his own cube train. Give the following directions for making cube trains:

- Make a cube train twenty cubes long; the cubes in the train must make a repeating pattern.
- When you're finished with the cube train, describe the repeating pattern to your teacher and a neighbor.
- Have your neighbor try to predict what color cube will come next in your train.

8. When students are finished making their cube trains, choose a few to show to the class. Have the students describe and make predictions about the cube trains, using the sentence frames for support.

9. Collect the students' cube trains. To keep track of the trains, put stickies on them, labeled with the students' names.

Day 2

Extending Patterns on the 1–100 Chart

1. Hold up one of the cube trains you modeled on Day 1 and have the class describe the pattern using the sentence frames for support.

2. Show the class a 1–100 chart. Using your train, model how to color in the 1–100 chart to show the repeating pattern on the cube train.

3. Introduce the words *vertical*, *horizontal*, and *diagonal*. Have the students describe and make predictions about the patterns on the 1–100 chart, using the sentence frames for support.

4. Give each student a 1–100 chart and provide the following directions:

+ Take your cube train back to your desk.
+ Color in the cube train pattern on your 1–100 chart.
+ Describe the cube train pattern to a neighbor.

5. When students are finished, choose a few 1–100 charts to show the class. Have the students describe and make predictions about the patterns on the charts, using the sentence frames for support. As students describe and make predictions, record their ideas on the board.

6. Direct students to write about the patterns on their 1–100 charts.

7 Junk Sorting

An Algebra Lesson

Day 1: Grades K, 1, and 2
Day 2: Grades 1 and 2

Overview

In this lesson, students learn to sort and categorize objects by their attributes. They begin by sorting objects into two groups and categorizing them by what they are and what they are not ("These are red and these are not red."). Students then sort and categorize the objects by four different attributes.

In a minilesson prior to the math lesson, students are introduced to vocabulary words and sentence frames that will help them when they explain their categories for sorting in the lesson.

Math Goal: Sort and categorize objects by different attributes

Language Goal: Categorize objects

Key Vocabulary: belong, category/categorize, colored, long, metal, names of the objects on the class chart, objects, plastic, round, sharp, short, soft, sort/sorting, wax, white, and wood

Materials

✦ colored pencils (or another set of familiar objects, such as crayons, that vary in only one attribute: color), several in each of 4 colors
✦ vocabulary word cards for *sort, sorting, category, categorize,* and *objects*

- pocket chart
- 5 sentence strips for sentence frames
- 12-by-18-inch construction paper, 1 piece per student
- 1 zip-top sandwich bag per student containing the following suggested items:

birthday candle	penny
spring-loaded clothespin	nickel
straw	crayon
colored counting chip	cotton ball
toothpick	cotton swab
screw	colored rubber band
metal washer	pencil
paper clip	colored plastic cube
color tile	

- class chart that includes each of the above items attached to it and their names

Sentence Frames That Help Students Categorize Their Sorts

Beginning

> Beginning ELLs would be expected to use a one-word response to describe how objects are sorted.

Intermediate and Advanced

> *These are _____. These are _____.*

> *These objects are _____. These objects are not _____.*

Sentence Frames That Help Students Explain Why Objects Belong in a Category

Beginning

> *The* _____ *is* _____ *(and* _____ *).*

Intermediate and Advanced

> *I put the* _____ *here because it is* _____ *(and* _____ *).*

> *The* _____ *belongs here because it is* _____ *(and* _____ *).*

Class Profile

Of the twenty students in Mary Kim's class, two are beginning English learners, five are intermediate-level English learners, and three are English learners with advanced fluency. The remaining students are native English speakers.

From the Classroom ◆ **Day 1: Sorting with Two Categories**

Minilesson Introducing Academic Language

Christine Sphar greeted the students in Mary Kim's class as they assembled in a semicircle on the rug in front of the room. To begin the minilesson, she took a handful of colored pencils and placed a few of them into two groups on the rug, with two blue pencils in one group and two red pencils in another group.

"I'm sorting the pencils," Christine said as she held up cards with the words *sort* and *sorting* on them. After students read the words aloud in a choral voice, Christine placed the word cards in a pocket chart and explained that when you sort things, you put them into groups. She then continued to place more blue and red pencils in the two groups on the rug. Christine used colored pencils to sort because they are familiar objects to the students.

"How am I sorting the pencils?" Christine asked the class. "Think for a second."

Christine gave the class some think time, then prompted them by saying, "The pencils are sorted by . . ."

"Color!" the students responded. Providing prompts and eliciting choral responses are two strategies that help English learners produce language.

Christine continued sorting the pencils, this time adding two more groups: yellow pencils and green pencils. Soon, she had four groups of pencils on the rug with about five pencils in each group. Christine had a few more pencils left in her hand and she asked a couple of volunteers to come up and place the pencils in the correct group. When all the pencils were sorted, Christine asked the class a question.

"How did I *sort* the pencils?" she asked, emphasizing the new word and pointing to it on the vocabulary chart.

"By color!" the students responded.

"I want you to think about why these pencils are in this group," Christine said, pointing to the blue pencils. "And why these are in this group," she continued, pointing to the green pencils, then the red ones, and finally to the yellow pencils. She held up cards with the words *category* and *categorize* written on them.

"When you *sort* things, you can *categorize* them," she told the class. "*Categorize* means that you decide *why* things, like the pencils, are in a group and you can *tell* someone why. We call that group a *category*."

Christine then pointed to each group and asked the students what color the pencils were. "Blue!" "Green!" "Red!" "Yellow!" they called out in unison.

"So I sorted the pencils by color, and the categories are blue, green, red, and yellow pencils," Christine explained. She then introduced the first sentence frame, reading it aloud to the class and then directing the students to read it together, pausing for the blank spaces. For younger children who are not yet reading, the sentence frames are used orally, modeled by the teacher and then practiced by the students.

These are _____. *These are* _____.

As she pointed to different groups of pencils, she had the students practice describing the categories.

"These are blue! These are green!"

"These are yellow! These are red!"

When they were finished practicing the frame, Christine used her open hand and waved it over all of the pencils. "What are these called?" she asked.

"Pencils!" the students replied.

Christine held up a card with the word *objects* written on it. She read it aloud and then had the students echo the word back. Christine knows that if she expects English language learners to use vocabulary words to describe their mathematical thinking, she needs to explicitly *teach* the words first.

"*Objects* is a fancy word for *things*," she said. "We'll make it fancier and call the pencils *objects*." Christine then introduced another sentence frame, reading it first to model and then directing the students to read it aloud together, pausing for the blank spaces.

> *These objects are _____. These objects are not _____.*

Pointing to the blue pencils and then the red ones, Christine modeled using the frame. "These objects are blue. These objects are not blue," she said.

Pointing to the pencils again, she had the class practice the frame with her. Then Christine called on a few volunteers to use the frames to talk about the categories.

Pointing first to the red group of pencils and then to the yellow group, Antonio said, "These objects are red. These objects are not red."

As volunteers practiced using the frames, some students found it easier to identify a category by what it was than to identify a category for what it was not. Most used the advanced frame to practice. Abel, an English learner with intermediate fluency, self-regulated and used the intermediate sentence frame because it was easier. "These are blue and these are not blue," he said, pointing to the blue group and then the yellow group of pencils.

Brittany, a native English speaker, modified the frame a bit, saying, "These are green, not blue, and these objects are yellow."

After putting away the colored pencils, Christine showed the class a piece of construction paper, folded it vertically in half to create two sections for sorting, then opened it and placed it on the rug in front of her. She told the students that this was her sorting mat. Then she held up a clear zip-top sandwich bag for the students to see. Inside the bag, there was a collection of objects.

"This is my junk bag," Christine told the students. "Junk is like things that we find around the house or at school when we're cleaning, extra stuff that we may not want anymore." To activate the students' prior knowledge, she spilled the objects onto the sorting mat and asked students to ＿＿＿＿＿＿＿ things they recognized.

When students w＿＿＿＿＿＿＿＿＿＿＿ d down from five to get their attention bac＿＿＿＿＿＿＿＿ m the names of the objects they saw.

"I see an unshar＿＿＿＿＿＿＿＿ tine was pleased that Jafir used an adjective＿＿＿＿＿＿ oted this aloud to the class. Christine is alw＿＿＿＿＿＿＿ to highlight language use in math class. Sh＿＿＿＿＿＿＿ math to English learners, she is also teach＿＿＿＿＿＿＿ *in* English.

"I see someth＿＿＿＿＿＿＿ ears with!" Antonio exclaimed. "What's＿＿＿＿＿

Christine wait＿＿＿＿＿＿＿ hen no one responded to Antonio's query＿＿＿＿＿ as called a *cotton swab*.

After the stud＿＿＿＿＿＿＿ objects as they could, Christine showed ＿＿＿＿＿＿＿ ach of the objects from the bag taped to i＿＿＿＿＿＿ e object (see illustration on next page).

One by one, ＿＿＿＿＿＿＿ em, saying its name and then directing th＿＿＿＿＿＿＿ e back to her. Next, she engaged the stud＿＿＿＿＿＿＿ rovide a context for learning the names o＿＿＿＿＿＿ out their attributes.

"I spy some＿＿＿＿＿＿ t is red," Christine told the class. "Can you ＿＿＿＿＿＿＿ king of?" She gave students a few seconds ＿＿＿＿＿＿＿ time gives English learners time to formula＿＿＿＿

"The red ＿＿＿＿＿＿＿＿＿＿

"I think it ＿＿＿＿＿＿＿＿ d.

"The colo＿＿＿＿＿

"All of th＿＿＿＿＿＿ hristine said, pointing to the items on the s＿＿＿＿＿＿ vhich one I'm thinking of? Did I give you enough informa＿＿＿

"No!" the students responded.

"OK. I'll give you another clue. I spy something red *and* square," Christine said, revealing two attributes rather than one. This time, lots of hands shot in the air.

"On three, let's all whisper the answer together," Christine directed. On three, everyone whispered, "Color tile!"

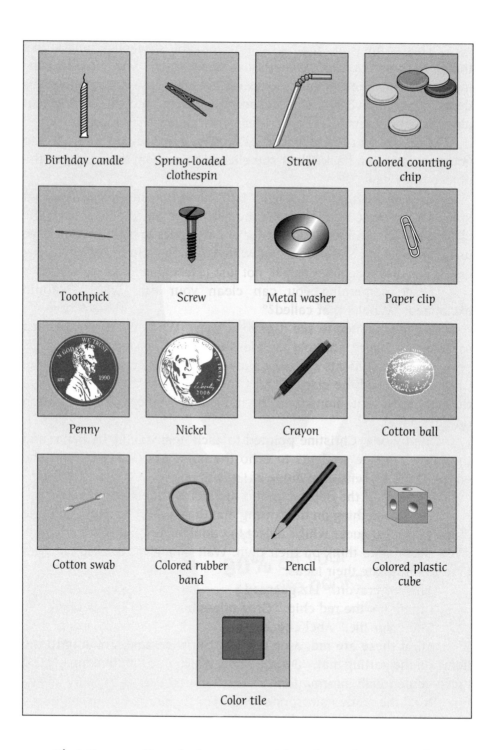

Birthday candle

Spring-loaded clothespin

Straw

Colored counting chip

Toothpick

Screw

Metal washer

Paper clip

Penny

Nickel

Crayon

Cotton ball

Cotton swab

Colored rubber band

Pencil

Colored plastic cube

Color tile

Christine continued the game with other objects, each time adding more clues until students all agreed on the identity of a single object. This helped them become familiar with the objects' names and their attributes: metal, wax, plastic, color, round, wooden, and so on.

The I spy game brought an end to the minilesson. The students had been introduced to key vocabulary, including the names and attributes of the objects they would be sorting, and sentence frames that would help them use the vocabulary in the upcoming lesson on sorting.

Introducing the Activity

Christine began the lesson by modeling a sort with the students. She started by placing a penny on one side of her sorting mat and a red cube and a red chip on the other.

"Do you know how I'm sorting the objects?" Christine asked the class.

"I think it's red and not red," Eduardo, an advanced English learner, posited. Lots of students nodded their heads in agreement.

"You're right, Eduardo," Christine acknowledged. "I'm sorting the objects by things that are red and things that are not red. Let's practice saying that together."

As she pointed to the intermediate-level sentence frame, Christine had the students say the words along with her as she pointed to one side of the sorting mat and then the other. "These are red. These are not red."

Next, Christine had the students practice the advanced frame.

"These objects are red. These objects are not red."

Christine then held up the nickel and asked the class where it belonged on the mat. She called on Abel.

"It goes there," he said, pointing to the side of the mat where the penny was.

"Why?" Christine probed.

"Because it is not red," Abel replied. "The nickel is not red."

"What about the straw?" Christine asked the class. To challenge students' thinking, she chose the straw, which was white with red stripes.

"I think it goes with the red stuff," Kay speculated. "It's part red, so it goes with the red."

Christine checked to see who agreed and who disagreed by asking for thumbs up or down. This nonverbal response gave the students with beginning and intermediate English proficiency a chance to participate without having to talk.

"It looks like some think it goes with the red and some disagree," Christine observed. "We'll put it with the reds, but it's tricky because the straw is part red, not all red."

Christine finished her first sort and then modeled two more sorts (metal vs. not metal and round vs. not round) for students to guess and then talk about using the sentence frames for support. When she was finished modeling, Christine had the students brainstorm ideas for sorting. Following is a list they came up with:

metal/not metal

white/not white

round/not round

silver/not silver

red/not red

wood/not wood

plastic/not plastic

things that burn/things that don't burn

things found in the bathroom/things not found in the bathroom

long things/short things

blue/not blue

wax/not wax

After recording their ideas on the board, Christine distributed to each student a piece of construction paper and a zip-top bag with objects inside. She had them fold their paper in half to create a sorting mat and then take the objects out and sort them into two groups.

The students enjoyed having their own sandwich bags and mats, and they were motivated to think of sorts on their own. As they worked, Christine made her way around the rug, checking in and encouraging students to talk about their sorts, using the sentence frames if needed.

"Blue, not blue," Mohammed said, showing his sort to Christine. Mohammed is a beginning English learner; he used the most basic frame to talk about how he categorized his objects.

"These are blue and these are not blue," Ghader noted to her partner.

Kay, an intermediate-level English learner, said, "These objects are straight and these objects are not straight." Christine was pleased that Kay stretched herself and used the advanced frame for support.

When most students had finished, Christine directed them to talk about their sorts with a partner if they hadn't already. Afterward, Christine regained students' attention and asked for a volunteer to share his or her sort. Marshal, an English learner with intermediate proficiency, scooted his mat up front so that everyone could clearly see it.

"Who can guess how Marshal sorted his junk?" Christine asked. She had the students turn to a partner and make a guess, giving them yet another opportunity to talk about their mathematical thinking.

After a few guesses from the class, Marshal explained his sort. "We can see through these ones," he said, pointing to the straw, rubber band, clothespin, and paper clip. "But we can't see through these ones." Listening to Marshal made Christine think about how *Junk Sorting* afforded students many opportunities to talk, think critically, and use their creativity.

After the students did one more sort, Christine wrapped up the lesson by giving specific directions for putting the junk away. She wanted to give the class another opportunity to think about the objects' attributes.

"Put everything that is metal in your sandwich bag."

"Put the objects that are wooden inside your sandwich bag."

"Put the junk that is round in your sandwich bag."

"Put everything that is made out of wax in your sandwich bag."

"Now put everything else inside your sandwich bag."

✦ Day 2: Sorting with Four Categories

Christine began Day 2 of the lesson by asking the students to remind her of what *sorting* means.

"You sorted the pencils yesterday," Abel said. "When my mom washes clothes, she gets them one by one; she sorts the clothes."

Christine was pleased that Abel was making a real-world connection. "Abel, when your mom sorts the clothes, how does she do it?"

"She puts the white ones together and the color ones together," he explained.

"So your mom sorts clothes by color," Christine summarized. "The categories are white and colors."

Christine then asked the students to look at the objects on the class chart and think about their attributes. As she elicited their ideas, she wrote them down on the board, next to the class list of objects:

wood	*straight*	*things that can burn*
metal	*blue*	*hard*

round	long	*things you can write with*
red	white	*things you find in the bathroom*
silver	wax	*plastic*

When she was finished writing, Christine had the students read the words on the list. She then drew a sketch of a sorting mat on the board, divided into four equal parts.

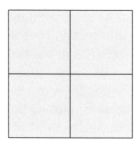

"What four things should we sort by?" she asked, pointing to the list of attributes on the board. She gave the students a few seconds to peruse the list again, and then she called on a few of them to choose. As they offered their ideas, Christine wrote the attributes inside the drawing of the sorting mat.

Wood	Metal
Wax	Plastic

To model the sort, Christine held up a toothpick and asked the students where she should put it. This was easy for them. To challenge their thinking, she held up the clothespin, which was part wood and part metal.

"I think it goes with the wood!" Ellen exclaimed.

"I think it should be both," Zuhra countered.

"For the clothespin, you'll have to decide for yourself," Christine told the class. "It's tricky, because there isn't a place on the sorting mat for an object that is part metal *and* part wood. You could put the clothespin with wood or metal; both would be correct."

After modeling a few more items, Christine distributed the zip-top bags and sorting mats to the students. She modeled how to fold the mat so that it was divided into four equal parts. Soon, the students were enthusiastically working on their new sort.

When they were finished, Christine regained their attention and introduced a new set of sentence frames. After reading each frame, Christine had the students read them aloud, pausing for the blank spaces.

> The _____ is _____ (and _____).

> I put the _____ here because it is _____ (and _____).

> The _____ belongs here because it is _____ (and _____).

To model how to use the frames, Christine held up the toothpick from Season's sorting mat and said, "The toothpick is made of wood." She had the students echo the sentence back to her. Christine then held up the washer and said, "The washer is metal." Again, the students echoed back.

Next, Christine modeled how to use the intermediate and advanced sentence frames, and the students practiced along with her. Picking up the candle, she said, "I put the candle here because it is wax." Continuing, she said, "I can also say, 'The candle belongs here because it is wax.'"

After modeling how to use the sentence frames, Christine had the students work with a partner and explain or justify their reasoning for placing their objects on the sorting mat. As the students shared, Christine listened in on a few partners.

"I put the crayon here because it is wax," Liz said.

"What about this one?" Christine asked, pointing to the cotton ball.

"I put the cotton ball in my bag 'cause it doesn't belong anywhere," Liz responded.

Holding up the rubber band, Jafir said, "This is not red, metal, long, or wood, so I put it on the table." Students will often use the sentence frames as a starting place and then expand their use of language on their own. The frames are there to support, not to restrict.

"I put this here because it is metal," Kay explained, using the intermediate sentence frame to show where she put the washer. "And I put the straw here because it is plastic."

Season, a native English speaker, used the advanced frame, saying, "The penny and the nickel belong here because they are made of metal."

Mohammed, an English learner with beginning skills, used the most basic frame to tell about the pencil. Pointing to the pencil, he said, "The pencil is wood."

After partners had time to talk about why they placed their objects in categories, Christine had them clear their sorting mats and elicited four different categories for a new sort.

Found in the Bathroom	Round
White	Blue

Once again, Christine modeled for the class how to do the sort and talk about it. She picked up an object from the bag, pointed to where it would go on the mat, and used the sentence frames to explain why the she placed it there. When she was finished giving several examples, Christine had the students work on their own.

This new sort prompted lots of interesting discussions among the students. For example, Isaac couldn't figure out whether the cotton ball would go with the round things, white things, or with the items found in the bathroom. He related a story about a time he went to the doctor's office and got a shot, requiring the nurse to rub his arm with a cotton ball. Ghader thought the candle belonged in the bathroom ("In case the lights go out!") *and* with the things that were white, so she decided to place the candle on the line between the two groups. *Junk Sorting* provided a rich context for using mathematical reasoning to problem solve. The activity also prompted students to develop and use their academic language *and* the informal English they use in everyday conversations.

When the students were finished with the sort, Christine had them clear their sorting mats and put their junk in the bags to prepare for the next part of the lesson.

A Challenge

Christine posted the chart from the previous day that listed the different ways the items could be sorted.

metal/not metal

white/not white

round/not round

silver/not silver

red/not red

wood/not wood

plastic/not plastic

things that burn/things that don't burn

things found in the bathroom/things not found in the bathroom

long things/short things

blue/not blue

wax/not wax

"These are some of the different ways we sorted the junk yester-day," Christine reminded the class. Together, they read the words on the chart. Next, Christine drew another picture of a sorting mat on the board. This time, she created a four-section matrix, so that it could be used to sort items by two attributes.

	Long	Not Long
Made of Wood		
Not Made of Wood		

To model the sort, Christine held up the color tile and asked the class, "Is the color tile made of wood?" This question was purposely designed for beginning-level English learners. It was simple and required a one-word response.

"No!" students responded.

"So it goes on this part of the sorting mat," Christine said, point-ing to the bottom half of the mat where the things not made of wood should go. She then asked, "Is the color tile long or not long?"

"Not long!" several students responded.

Pointing to the lower right-hand corner of the matrix, and using the sentence frames to model, Christine said, "I can say I put the color tile here because it is not long and not made of wood. Or, I can say the color tile belongs here because it is not long and not made of wood."

Christine modeled this new, challenging sort a few more times. The students practiced along with her each time she used the sentence frames to explain or justify why an object belonged in a certain category. When she was finished modeling, Christine directed the students to complete the sort on their own, using their sorting mats and the junk in their bags.

Sorting with a four-section matrix was very difficult for the students, and most needed some initial assistance. Christine made her way around the class, helping individuals and then encouraging them to help their partners. For support, Christine first asked a student to choose an item from her bag.

"Where does the pencil go on your sorting mat?" she asked Liz.

Liz thought for a minute, looking confused.

"Is the pencil made of wood or not made of wood?" Christine queried, helping Liz focus on one attribute at a time.

"Wood," Liz responded. Looking up at the beginning sentence frame, she continued, "The pencil is made of wood."

Christine then pointed to the half of Liz's sorting mat where wooden objects would go and asked, "Is the pencil long or not long?"

"The pencil is long," Liz responded.

Christine prompted, "The pencil is long and . . ."

"The pencil is long and made out of wood," Liz said.

Liz began to catch on and finally figured out where on her sorting mat the pencil belonged. Christine encouraged her to use the sentence frames to explain why she placed the pencil where she did.

"I put the pencil here because it is wood and it is long," Liz reasoned.

Thinking about two attributes was tricky for Liz and for many of her classmates. Christine knew, however, that they would improve with practice.

When most of the students were finished with the sort, Christine called for their attention. She directed them to work with a partner and use the sentence frames to explain why their objects belonged in a category. Then she posed a new sort for them to work on by drawing another four-section matrix on the board.

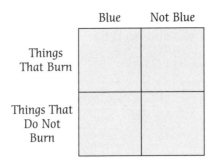

	Blue	Not Blue
Things That Burn		
Things That Do Not Burn		

Although the sort was still challenging, students had a much easier time with the four-section matrix the second time around. As students worked on their sort, Christine walked around, urging students to explain their reasoning.

"Why did you put the clothespin there?" Christine asked Ghader.

"The clothespin is not blue and you can burn it," she said, referring to the sentence frame for support.

"The clothespin belongs here because it is wood and it can actually burn," Isaac explained. "It's not even blue!"

"Why did you put the washer there?" Christine asked him.

"Well, I put the washer here because it can't burn," he replied. "And it's not blue. But it could burn you if you got it hot!"

Moving on to Kay, Christine inquired, "Why did you put the paper clip there?"

Kay, an English learner with intermediate fluency, responded, "It's not blue and it's not burn."

Christine acknowledged that Kay was indeed correct, then paraphrased to model correct syntax. "It's not blue and it does not burn."

When she thought students had had enough time to finish their sorts and talk about them, Christine brought an end to *Junk Sorting* by collecting the materials.

Reflecting on the lesson, Christine was impressed by the language students were able to use to explain their mathematical thinking. She also thought about ways she could adjust the lesson if students needed more support.

Modifications for Younger Children

- Teach Day 1 only.
- Teach Day 1 and Day 2, but leave out the challenging four-section matrix.
- Teach parts of the lesson in small groups.

◆ Use the sentence frames orally, especially for those students who are not yet able to read.

◆ **Junk Sorting**

Day 1

Minilesson Introducing Academic Language

1. Introduce the words *sort, sorting, category,* and *categorize.* Explain to students what each word means.

2. Show the students an assortment of colored pencils (or another set of familiar objects that vary in only one attribute). Begin by putting the pencils in groups based on their color. Invite several volunteers to come up to finish the sort by placing a pencil in the appropriate group. As you and the students are sorting the pencils, introduce the following sentence frames, using them to model how to categorize the sorts, and have the students practice using them:

Beginning

> Beginning ELLs would be expected to use a one-word response to describe how objects are sorted.

Intermediate and Advanced

> *These are (_____). These are (_____).*

> *These objects are (_____). These objects are not (_____).*

3. Take a bag containing a variety of objects and spill the contents on a sorting mat for all students to see. Direct partners to talk about the objects and try to name the ones that they recognize.

4. Referring to a class chart, introduce the objects and their names, one at a time. Direct the students to say the name of each object aloud in a choral voice.

5. To further familiarize the students with the names and attributes of each of the objects in the bag, play a game of I spy. Begin with an object that will require just two or three descriptions.

Teacher: I spy something that is round. What is the object? (*Students will give varied responses and soon discover that they need more information.*)

Teacher: I spy something that is round and is silver. (*Students all agree that it is a nickel.*)

Continue the game with other objects. Keep adding clues until students all agree on the identity of a single object.

Introducing the Activity

1. Model a sort with the students. First, fold the sorting mat in half. Then tell the students that you want to sort the objects into two groups (e.g., metal and not metal). Hold up one object at a time and ask the students whether the object is made of metal or not. With student direction, place each object in the correct group on the sorting mat.

2. When all objects have been sorted into two groups on the sorting mat, direct the students to use the sentence frames introduced in the minilesson to help them categorize the sorts.

3. Repeat the process using another rule for sorting (white vs. not white, long vs. short, round vs. not round, etc.).

4. Elicit from students different ways to sort the objects into two groups and record their ideas on the board.

5. Distribute a sorting mat (piece of construction paper) to each student. Have the students fold their sorting mats in half.

6. Distribute a bag of objects to each student, have them take the objects out of their bags, and direct them to sort their objects into two groups. Once they are finished, students should try to guess how their partner's objects are sorted, using the sentence frames for support.

7. Give directions for putting the objects back into the bags by suggesting specific attributes. For example:

   ◆ Put everything that is white in your bag.
   ◆ Put all the metal objects in your bag.
   ◆ Put anything that is soft in your bag.
   ◆ Put all the round objects in your bag.

Day 2

Sorting with Four Categories

1. Distribute a sorting mat to each student. Have them fold the mat into four equal parts. On the board, draw a picture of the sorting mat:

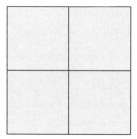

2. Show students the class chart displaying the objects for sorting and their names. Brainstorm different attributes for categorizing or sorting the objects (wood, metal, wax, etc.), and record their ideas on the board.

3. Choose four attributes from the brainstormed list and record an attribute in each of the four sections on the sorting mat drawn on the board.

Wood	Metal
Wax	Plastic

4. Distribute a bag of objects to each student and have them complete the sort. Introduce the following sentence frames by picking up one of the items on a student's sorting mat and describing the object by an attribute (e.g., "The clothespin is wood."). Then tell why the object is placed in a certain category (e.g., "I put the clothespin here because it is wood," or "The clothespin belongs here because it is wood.").

Beginning

The _____ is _____ (and _____).

> *I put the _____ here because it is _____ (and _____).*

> *The _____ belongs here because it is _____ (and _____).*

5. Model this process for several objects, and then have students practice with a partner using the objects on their own sorting mats. Partners discuss the objects and categories, using the sentence frames for support.

6. Choose four different attributes and have students complete another sort and discuss it with their partners.

7. Show students how to fold their mats into a four-section matrix so that it can be used to sort items by two attributes. Draw the following four-section matrix on the board, placing the headings outside the sections:

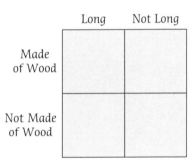

While working on this sort, students may discover that they have some objects that will not fit the limits of the headings and will therefore belong outside the matrix.

8. When students are finished with the sort, extend the sentence frames that were introduced in Step 4. Model the frames by picking up one of the items on a student's sorting mat and describing the object using two of its attributes (e.g., "The clothespin is wood and long.") and telling why the object is placed in a certain category (e.g., "I put the clothespin here because it is wood and long," or "The clothespin belongs here because it is wood and long.").

9. Model this process for several objects, and then have students practice with a partner using the objects on their own sorting mats.

Partners discuss the objects and categories, using the sentence frames for support.

10. Draw a new four-section matrix on the board using different categories (e.g., round, not round and metal, not metal; white, not white and wood, not wood). Have students complete this sort and then talk about it with their partners.

Helping English Language Learners Make Sense of Math Word Problems 8

English language learners (ELLs) typically experience difficulty understanding and therefore solving math word problems for a variety of reasons. Word problems require more careful and slower reading than other prose because of the technical words and symbols and the heavy load of concepts that they present (Carrasquilo and Segan 1998). Consider the following problem:

> *The greatest amount of honey Mr. Morgan's bees ever made in one week was 6 pounds. The least amount of honey his bees ever made in one week was 2 pounds. What is the difference between the greatest and least amount of honey the bees made in a week?*

This relatively short paragraph is packed with information that a student needs to understand in order to figure the answer. Throughout the problem, the reader confronts and has to make sense of a variety of concept words related to mathematics: *greatest amount, least amount, pounds, difference, between,* and *week.*

Vocabulary used in math word problems is another source of difficulty for English language learners. Understanding vocabulary is crucial; almost every word, number, and symbol carries important meaning, and misunderstanding just one word in a story problem can prevent an ELL from finding a solution. English learners can become confused if the mathematics vocabulary has different meanings in everyday usage, as with *even, odd, difference, function,* and *operation.* Words such as *sum* and *whole* can also cause confusion for English learners because they have nonmathematical homonyms.

Another obstacle is with an incomplete understanding of syntax and grammar. For example, word problems are often embedded in language that makes the problems unclear or difficult to comprehend. Consider the following problem:

Tina's mom brought 3 packs of soda to the party.
Each pack had 6 sodas.
How many sodas did she bring to the party?

This word problem uses both the past and present tenses of the irregular verb *to bring* in one question, which may cause difficulty for an ELL, depending on the student's English language proficiency. In addition, the use of the possessive *Tina's mom* could be confusing to English learners if possessives are not used in their native language, as in Spanish (in Spanish, *Tina's mom* would read *la mamá de Tina*, or, *the mother of Tina*). Also, the word used to describe the grouping of sodas is *pack*, another multiple-meaning word that may not be common to the working vocabulary of an English language learner.

In addition to the linguistic demands presented by math word problems, English language learners must also contend with the specific details included in each problem. In theory, these details provide a context for the problem. In reality, they often serve to further obfuscate the question being posed. While the purpose for the details is to create a context that is more applicable to real-life mathematical situations than straight computation, the inadvertent results are contexts that may be completely unrelated to the lives of ELLs. The following problem illustrates how the context of a math word problem can carry a cultural bias:

The Scouts clean the trailhead parking lot each spring. There are 28 Scouts who have signed up for the cleanup. If the Scouts are evenly divided among 7 groups, how many are in each group?

The details in this problem make sense to someone who participates in children's service organizations and spends time hiking. While these details are often cumbersome even for native English speakers, English language learners may find them foreign and intimidating.

Some English language learners, especially those with beginning- or intermediate-level skills, will need help understanding the language used in math word problems. Once this barrier of language is lifted, English learners should be able to successfully focus on the mathematics and solve the problem. Other English learners, especially those who also struggle with mathematics, may need support with language *and* math.

Whatever language or math skills your English learners possess, it is important that students have opportunities to make sense of the mathematics in their own way once the barrier of language is lifted.

Strategies to Help English Learners Make Sense of Math Word Problems

Following is a list of teaching strategies that can help all students, especially English language learners, make sense of and solve math word problems. Determining which strategy to use depends upon the word problem being posed.

- ✦ Read the word problem aloud to students before showing them a printed version. This is especially important for young children who are not yet reading. Hearing the problem read aloud also helps students focus on visualizing the problem.
- ✦ Have students practice reading the problem aloud together, and then ask the following questions:

  What do you know?

  Is anything confusing (words, phrases)?

  What do you have to find out?

  What numbers and operations will you use to solve the problem?

- ✦ Use synonyms for unfamiliar words (e.g., names of people and places).
- ✦ Identify multiple-meaning words and homophones (words that are pronounced in the same way but have different meanings and sometimes spellings) and clarify their meanings.
- ✦ Model retelling the problem using synonyms or gestures for difficult words, and then have students practice retelling the problem.
- ✦ Act out the problem or use realia (e.g., money) to model the problem.

- Draw a picture or chart to help students visualize the problem and/or have students sketch a picture of their solution strategy.
- Ask students clarifying questions, and then have them go back to the text to prove their answers.
- Help students become aware of complex or difficult syntax.
- Help students identify what the numbers stand for in the problem.
- Have students write their own word problems, providing sentence frames and a vocabulary bank for support.
- Pose word problems in contexts that are familiar to students.

Word Problems in Kindergarten

To help her kindergartners make sense of math word problems, Amy Vadagama consistently uses several strategies. Her word problems are always situated in contexts that are familiar to her students and she uses realia to make the problems visible. She retells the problems orally several times before having the students retell and then solve the problems. Amy provides manipulative materials so that students can model the problems, and she makes sure that students have opportunities to talk with a partner.

Of the eighteen students in Amy's class, half are native English speakers, and the other half are English language learners with a range of proficiency levels from beginning to advanced. The native languages spoken by her students include English, Spanish, Cambodian, Somali, Swahili, and Laotian.

Before she began a lesson on a word problem involving bags of candy, Amy instructed half the students to each get a little white dry-erase board, a black marker, and an eraser and bring them to the rug. She told the other half of the class to each get a small plastic container with interlocking cubes inside and a piece of colored construction paper on which to place their cubes while working. As the students brought their materials to the rug area, Amy had them arrange themselves so that every other student had a dry-erase board or a container of cubes.

"Tools down, eyes on me," Amy instructed. The students followed her directions and were eager to get started.

"I have a math problem for you to solve," Amy began. She held up two clear plastic zip-top bags; inside each bag were two pieces of candy. Amy likes to use real objects from the environment when posing word problems because these visuals help English learners see basic concepts and give meaning to the words in the problems.

"Do you see my two bags?" Amy asked. "Inside each bag I have two pieces of candy. How many *pieces of candy* do I have?" Amy repeated the word problem aloud and then had the students turn to a partner and talk about how they would solve it.

In the early and middle parts of the school year, Amy poses word problems orally as opposed to showing students a problem written down on chart paper. Later in the year, when more students are reading, she will present problems orally and in written form. Amy also spends a lot of time during the year explicitly teaching and reteaching her students how to conduct partner talk. The procedures that students follow when talking with a partner are posted in clear view on one of the classroom walls:

1. Students sit knee-to-knee.
2. Eyes on each other.
3. One talks, one listens.
4. Ask questions.
5. Take turns.

After partners had time to talk about their plan, the students got to work solving the problem. Some used the whiteboards and interlocking cubes, while others counted on their fingers. After a couple of minutes, Amy counted down from three to zero to regain the students' attention. She then called on volunteers to share their thinking.

"Tools down, eyes on Amanda," Amy directed.

"It's four," Amanda began. Amanda is a student with intermediate-level skills in English. "It's four because, 'cause you do this." Amanda held up two fingers on one hand and two fingers on the other hand.

"And how do you know that it's four?" Amy asked.

"I counted them! One, two, three, four!" Amanda exclaimed, holding up her fingers and counting by ones.

"Thumbs up if you counted to find out how many candies there are," Amy said to the class. Asking for nonverbal responses from students gives those who are just beginning to learn English a chance to participate without having to produce language.

"Who thought of it a different way?" Amy asked the class.

"It's 'cause two and two makes four," Raya, a native English speaker, offered, showing the class two groups of two interlocking cubes pushed together to make four.

"So Raya joined a group of two and a group of two together to make four," Amy paraphrased.

When no one else had a different idea to share, Amy called on a volunteer to count the candies in the two plastic bags to verify the answer. Then she posed the next word problem for the children to solve.

"I have two bags," Amy began, holding up two plastic zip-top bags.

To make sure students understood, she asked the class, "How many bags do I have?"

"Two!" the students answered.

"*In each bag* I have three pieces of candy," Amy continued, pointing to the candies in each of the bags and emphasizing the words *in each bag*. "How many *pieces of candy* do I have altogether?"

The English learners in Amy's class often struggle with understanding the meaning of the words *in each* and *altogether*. Using realia and posing problems in familiar contexts (e.g., candies in bags) can help students with these difficult words. Using synonyms (e.g., *in every* for *in each* and *in all* for *altogether*) also facilitates understanding.

Amy repeated the word problem two more times and then had the students retell the problem to a partner before getting to work. As the students worked on the problem, Amy knew she would have only a couple of minutes before the class was finished solving the problem, so she sat down with one pair of students to observe and listen as they explained their thinking.

José is a student with very beginning English language skills and Bryan has intermediate-level proficiency in English. Amy first watched Bryan as he snapped three cubes together and placed them on one side of his construction paper. Next, he snapped another three cubes together and put them on the other side of his paper. He then put one cube next to each train of three cubes.

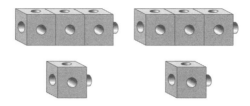

"Tell me about the problem, Bryan," Amy began.

"There are two bags of candy and there are three candies in the bags," Bryan explained.

"Three candies altogether or three candies in each bag?" Amy asked, attempting to help Bryan clarify.

"Three candies in each bag," Bryan stated.

"Bryan, what are these?" Amy asked, pointing to the single cubes next to each group of three. Amy wanted Bryan to articulate what the cubes stood for in the problem.

"Those are the bags," Bryan replied.

"And these?" Amy asked, pointing to the two trains with three cubes in each train.

"Those are the candies."

"So how many candies are there altogether?" Amy queried.

At first, Bryan sat there without responding. Amy helped out by prompting him with some sequence words. Sometimes English learners need verbal prompts to produce language. Without those verbal cues, English learners sometimes become stuck and are unable to articulate their thinking.

"First . . . ," she said.

"First I put three cubes," he said.

"Then . . . ," Amy prompted again.

"Then I put three more cubes," he continued. "Then I said three, and I counted four, five, six. It's six candies." With the help of Amy's verbal prompts, Bryan was able to explain how he solved the problem.

"So you counted on," Amy observed, putting a name to Bryan's strategy.

Amy then turned to José, who had drawn two groups of three circles, representing candies, on his whiteboard.

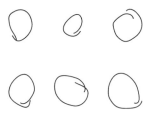

"What did you do?" Amy asked, starting with an open-ended question to see how José would respond.

"I put these," José said, pointing to the circles he'd drawn on his whiteboard.

Amy then asked more pointed questions that were designed for beginning English language learners. These questions required only a one-word response.

"What are they?" she inquired, pointing to his drawing.

"Candies," José answered.

"How many here?" Amy asked, pointing to the top row of circles.

"Three."

"And how many here?" Amy continued, pointing to the other row of three circles.

"Three," José replied.

"How many candies altogether?" Amy asked, using her hand to indicate both groups of three candies.

José started with the top row and counted, "One, two, three." He then continued counting the circles in the other row, and again said, "One, two, three."

Amy wasn't sure what José was having difficulty with. Was he struggling to join two groups of three candies? Was he experiencing difficulty with counting in English? Or did he misinterpret her question and think she wanted him to tell her how many candies there were in each bag? To check, Amy repeated her question and told José that he could tell her in his native language, Spanish.

José successfully counted in Spanish as he touched each circle that stood for the candies, "Uno, dos, tres, cuatro, cinco, seis."

When he was finished, Amy modeled counting the total in English and then had José do the counting in English. Using a student's native language as a resource can provide a window into a student's mathematical thinking. In this case, José showed that he could indeed join the two groups of candies and find the total. However, Amy knew that José would continue to need more modeling and practice with counting and explaining his thinking in English.

When she was finished with Bryan and José, Amy brought the class back together and had a few student volunteers share their thinking with the class. After that, she had the students switch math tools; students with the dry-erase boards and markers traded with those who had the cubes. Then Amy posed another problem for students to solve using their new tools:

This time I have three bags.
In each bag I have two pieces of candy.
How many candies do I have in all?

When students were finished working and after several volunteers shared their thinking, Amy posed a final problem for students to solve back at their seats:

I have three bags.
In each bag there are four pieces of candy.
How many candies do I have altogether?

As with the previous three word problems of the day, the problem context remained the same: candies in bags. Using the same context (but with different numbers) over and over helps English learners become familiar with the language in the problems and allows them to focus more on the mathematics. Figures 8–1 through 8–3 show how three students solved the last problem.

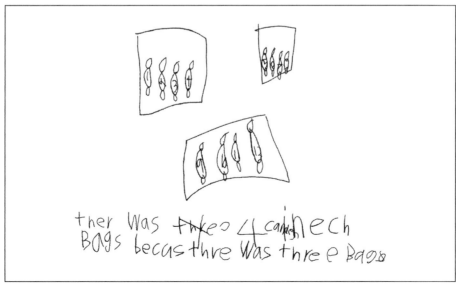

ther Was three 4 candy ech
Bags becus thre Was three Bags

FIGURE 8-1. Tith is a student whose native language is English. She is beginning to use written words to describe her math thinking.

FIGURE 8-2. Bryan is a student with intermediate fluency in English. He used pictures and numbers to help him correctly solve the word problem.

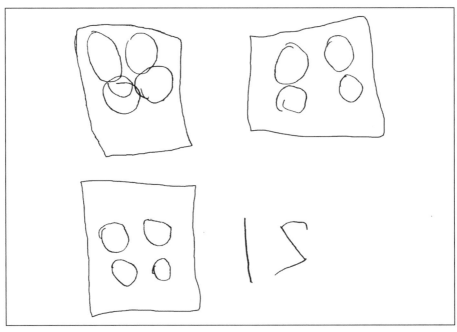

FIGURE 8-3. José is the beginning English learner who struggled with one of the previous problems while working with Amy. Here, he successfully found the total number of candies.

Word Problems in First Grade

Sharon Fargason poses word problems for her first graders to solve a couple of times a week. She typically has her class meet on the rug in the front of the room, where Sharon introduces the problem orally.

Reading problems orally is important in kindergarten and first grade, because not all children are able to read the problems on their own.

After Sharon reads the problem or tells the story, the students talk about the problem. They discuss what they know, talk about what they need to figure out, retell the story in their own words, and sometimes act out the problem. Sharon then dismisses the students back to their seats to solve the problem. During work time, the students have access to manipulative materials to use if they need them. When they are finished working on the problem, Sharon calls them back to the rug to share their solution strategies.

Of the twenty students in Sharon's class, all but one is an English language learner. Two students are beginning English speakers, eight have intermediate fluency, nine are advanced English speakers, and one student is a native English speaker.

Introducing the Word Problem

Sharon began by telling her students that she had a problem for them to solve and that it was a true story about Ms. Williams, another teacher at the school. This piqued the students' interest. Sharon likes to pose word problems in familiar contexts because the situations are easier for English language learners to make sense of and make connections to.

"Ms. Williams wants to buy something," Sharon began. "She's going on a field trip and she knows that her students will need something to protect them from the sun, so she decides to buy some visors."

Sharon held up two visors she had brought from home, a red one and a blue one. Sharon finds that using realia helps students understand words and their meanings.

"So Ms. Williams is at the store and there is a sale going on and things are less expensive than usual. Ms. Williams wants to buy the visors *now*. She has twenty students in her class, but she knows she always gets more students during the year, so she'll have to buy *more* than twenty visors. She wants to buy some blue visors and some red visors. She buys nine red visors. We want to figure out how many blue visors she should buy."

Sharon knew that the word problem she just told was too long for her students to remember. One strategy Sharon uses is to start with a longer, more embellished version to draw in students' attention. Then, she tells a much shorter account before she has the students retell.

Following is the shorter version Sharon told as a follow-up to her lengthy story:

Ms. Williams bought visors for her class.
She bought more than 20 visors.
She bought 9 red visors and some blue visors.
How many blue visors did she buy?

"Turn to a partner and talk about what you know about the problem," Sharon told the class. After about fifteen seconds, she called for the students' attention and elicited their ideas.

"She's going on a trip," Ashley said.

"She wants to buy visors," Oscar added.

"What's another word we could use for *visors*?" Sharon asked, pointing to the visors she had brought in.

"Hats!" students chorused. Sharon wrote the words *visor* and *hat* on the board. Using synonyms for unfamiliar words can be helpful to ELLs.

"What else do we know?" Sharon asked.

"She wants to buy visors!" Ayomide said.

Sharon noticed that Ayomide's idea was the same as the one Oscar had made moments earlier. Rather than inhibit these repetitive comments, Sharon welcomes them and is glad when students volunteer to share their thinking in English.

"Yes, but how many visors? How many *red* visors did she buy?" Sharon queried. After waiting several seconds to give her students think time, she called on Gurkan.

"Nine red visors," Gurkan reported.

"Say *nine red visors*!" Sharon directed the class.

"Nine red visors!" students chorused.

"Hold up nine fingers and say *nine red visors*!" Sharon instructed. The students giggled, then echoed back Sharon's words with their fingers in the air.

When the class settled, Sharon asked, "Who can retell the story for us?" She waited a few seconds until many hands were raised and then called on Dariana.

"She's going to a field trip," Dariana began. "And it might be sunny so she's going to buy visors. She might get more students, so she has to buy more than twenty."

"More than twenty," Sharon repeated, gesturing with her hands to show *more* by starting with them folded and then spreading them out. Sharon directed the students to motion with their hands as she had and say, "More than twenty!"

"Ms. Williams might have more than twenty students when she goes on the field trip so she needs to buy more than twenty visors," Sharon said, paraphrasing Dariana. "What's a number that's *more* than twenty? How many visors does she need?"

Pointing to the students in the class, Sharon continued, "You can decide on how many she needs."

Since the students would each be choosing their own total number of visors that Ms. Williams would be buying when solving the problem, Sharon wanted to make sure that they had a sense about which numbers would be reasonable. So she elicited several possibilities from students, ranging from twenty-one to thirty, and recorded them on the board. To help them think about numbers, some students referred to the 1–100 chart Sharon had posted in her room. This visual tool provided access to the math content for these students.

Acting Out the Word Problem

Next, Sharon held up a blue visor and a red visor and said, "We're going to act out the story and pretend that we're at the store."

The children were excited about playing store, and when Sharon asked for a volunteer to play the part of Ms. Williams, everyone's hand was raised, even the boys. Sharon played the part of the store-keeper, and she called on Daniel to be Ms. Williams. The students giggled.

"Good afternoon, Ms. Williams!" Sharon exclaimed, greeting Daniel with a smile. On chart paper near her, Sharon had written these four sentences:

How many visors do you need?
I need _____ visors.
How many red visors do you need?
I need _____ red visors.

Pointing to the words in the first sentence, Sharon asked Daniel, a student with intermediate fluency in English, "How many visors do you need?"

As she pointed to the second sentence, she helped Daniel reply, "I need . . . visors."

"So how many do you need? How many are you going to buy?" Sharon asked Daniel again.

"Twenty-five," Daniel said.

"Why twenty-five?" Sharon probed.

"Because it's more than twenty," he explained.

"How many red visors do you need?" Sharon asked, pointing to the sentence on the chart.

"Nine," Daniel replied.

"I need . . . ," Sharon prompted, pushing for more language.

"I need nine red visors," Daniel responded.

"So you want to buy twenty-five visors—nine red ones, and you have to figure out how many blue ones!" Sharon told him.

After calling a few more students up to play the part of Ms. Williams, Sharon had the students pair up, think about the total number of visors they wanted to buy, and then use the sentences introduced on chart paper to practice with a partner. Sharon's purpose for the playacting was to help the students understand and practice the words, visualize the situation, and remember the numbers in the story, not to give away strategies for solving the problem.

Observing the Students

When the students were finished with playacting, Sharon gave each student a sheet of paper with the word problem written on it and dismissed them to their seats.

As Sharon observed her students at work, she realized that the problem was tricky for them to solve and required a bit of decision making. They knew how many red visors they would get, but they had to decide on the total number of visors and figure out the number of blue visors. As Sharon circulated, she was pleased that the strategies she used to introduce the word problem had helped the students understand what the problem was about and the questions they had to answer.

Sharon first visited Buruj, a student with advanced fluency and strong math skills, whose native language is Somali. She watched as Buruj drew three circles, one large one and two smaller ones connected to the larger circle. Inside the larger circle, Buruj wrote the number 29. Inside one of the smaller circles, she wrote the number 9.

"I know that twenty plus nine is twenty-nine," she said to Sharon. To show that twenty-nine is indeed greater than twenty, Buruj wrote a number sentence at the bottom of her paper using a greater than symbol, which she'd learned about previously in class. (See Figure 8–4.)

Miss Williams wants to buy visors for everyone in her class to wear on their next field trip. The store has red visors and blue visors. She is not sure how many visors to buy in all, but she knows that if she buys more than 20, she will have enough. She chooses 9 red visors. How many blue visors should she take?

FIGURE 8–4. Buruj chose 29 as the total number of visors. She recorded the total, the number of red visors, and the missing addend.

Before moving on to another student, Sharon asked Buruj three questions:

- ◆ "Which number stands for the total number of visors Ms. Williams bought?"
- ◆ "Which number stands for the number of red visors she bought?"
- ◆ "Which number stands for the number of blue visors?"

Sharon worked with Axel next. Axel is a beginning English language learner who has strong math skills. Sharon spent most of her time helping Axel with the language in the word problem. She once again used the visors to review the situation and the numbers involved. She was providing the linguistic access that Axel needed in order to solve the problem. Once he understood, Axel quickly used mental math to figure the answer. Sharon is careful not to allow a student's struggles with language mask good math thinking. (See Figure 8–5.)

Dariana, a student with advanced fluency in English, solved the problem like most of the students in the class. She drew pictures to show the total number of visors to be bought, then colored in the nine red visors. Finally, she colored in the remaining visors to find the number of blue visors needed. (See Figure 8–6.)

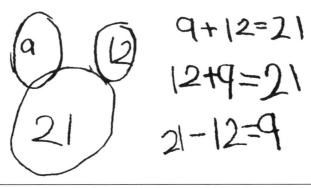

Miss Williams wants to buy visors for everyone in her class to wear on their next field trip. The store has red visors and blue visors. She is not sure how many visors to buy in all, but she knows that if she buys more than 20, she will have enough. She chooses 9 red visors. How many blue visors should she take?

FIGURE 8-5.
After getting help with the words in the problem, Axel quickly used mental math to solve the problem.

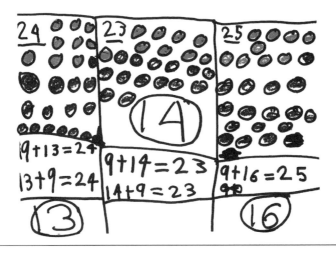

Miss Williams wants to buy visors for everyone in her class to wear on their next field trip. The store has red visors and blue visors. She is not sure how many visors to buy in all, but she knows that if she buys more than 20, she will have enough. She chooses 9 red visors. How many blue visors should she take?

FIGURE 8-6.
Dariana found two correct solutions to the problem using pictures and numbers.

Felipe is a student with beginning English skills who struggles with mathematics. As with Axel, Sharon had to provide a lot of linguistic support in order for Felipe to understand the language in the problem. But unlike Axel, Felipe also needed math support. To provide some scaffolding, Sharon adjusted the numbers in the problem for Felipe. For example, she changed the numbers from more than twenty to ten total visors needed and the number of red visors needed from nine to five. This created a much more manageable problem for Felipe to tackle.

When the students were finished working, Sharon brought them to the rug to discuss their solution strategies. This brought an end to math class for the day.

Word Problems in Second Grade

A couple of times a week, Alison Williams poses math word problems for her second graders to solve. She begins by gathering her class on the rug. Once the students are seated in a circle, Alison places several zip-top bags on the rug in reach of the children. Inside the bags are manipulative materials: color tiles, base ten blocks, interlocking cubes, toy dinosaurs, and so on. Alison refers to these manipulatives as "math tools." Manipulatives serve a variety of purposes and are important tools that can make math content comprehensible to ELLs. Manipulatives give students ways to construct physical models of abstract mathematical ideas; they build students' confidence by giving them a way to test and confirm their reasoning; they are useful tools for solving problems; and they make learning math interesting and enjoyable.

Although manipulatives can be useful in the hands of learners, they can also pose management challenges for the teacher. For this reason, Alison leads a brief conversation about how to use the tools before posing a word problem. She usually begins by asking the students to remind her about how the tools should be used. Students typically remind one another to

+ share the math tools;
+ use the tools for math and not for playing;
+ stop using the tools when someone is explaining her or his thinking;
+ listen for a signal from the teacher to put the tools away; and
+ put away the tools safely, quickly, and quietly.

Helping English Language Learners Make Sense of Math Word Problems

In Alison's class, there is the full range of English learners from beginning to advanced, including a few native English speakers. Native languages spoken by the students include English, Vietnamese, Spanish, Somali, and Laotian.

Posing Word Problems as Warm-Ups

"We're going to begin math class with a warm-up word problem," Alison told the class. "Who can tell us what we do after I tell the story problem?"

"You tell us a story, and we have to tell it back three times," Ricardo said.

"That's right," Alison acknowledged. "I tell the story, and then I call on three different people to retell it in their own words. That way, you all get four chances to understand the story problem." Having the students retell the story problems gives English learners access to the math content because everyone gets a chance to hear the problem explained in multiple ways, possibly with simpler syntax and vocabulary.

Alison generally presents word problems orally during the warm-ups because she finds that listening to the problem requires the students to pay close attention and focus on the words.

"Does everyone who retells the story have to say it in the exact same way I do?" Alison asked.

"No," Tommy replied. "We can use different words. But it has to be the same story."

Alison then posed the following word problem to the class:

Yesterday I went to the park. There were 5 benches. There were 2 people sitting on each bench. How many people were there altogether?

"Do you know what *benches* are?" Alison asked, making sure that students understood the meaning of this important word in the problem.

"They're like things to sit on, like chairs," Thomas said.

"We have benches at school to sit on when we eat lunch!" Jessica exclaimed.

Alison drew a quick sketch of a bench on the board and wrote the word *bench* next to the illustration. Whenever possible, Alison uses visuals to assist English learners.

Alison told the story again, and then asked the students to think of another word that means the same as *each. Each* is another key word in the story problem, one that students would have to understand in order to solve the problem correctly.

"Every!" students chorused.

"So there were two people sitting on *each* bench," Alison reminded, emphasizing the word *each*. "Or, we could say that there were two people sitting on *every* bench."

Alison then had the students pair up and retell the word problem in their own words, thereby giving everyone an opportunity to think through the problem. Partner talk is an important strategy because it gives students time to rehearse. When they were finished, she asked three volunteers to share. Yareli went first.

"When you go to the park you see five benches and two people on each benches," she began. When it was evident that Yareli was having difficulty remembering the rest of the problem, Alison provided some help.

"So when I went to the park, I saw five benches and there were two people on each bench," Alison paraphrased, modeling correct grammar. "What do I want to know?" Alison asked. "What's the question we have to answer?" Figuring out the question to be answered in word problems is difficult for the students in Alison's class, especially for the ELLs.

"How many people were on the benches?" Yareli asked in an uncertain tone.

"That's right!" Alison responded.

After listening to two more students retell the story, Alison directed the class to start working on the problem. As they worked, she made her way around the circle of students, observing and taking mental notes about the strategies that they were using. When the students were finished, Alison called for their attention and asked for volunteers to explain how they solved the word problem.

Sharing Strategies

When Alison asked for volunteers to share their solution strategies, nearly everyone's hand flew into the air. Alison has worked hard to create a safe learning environment, one in which students feel safe to make mistakes. So it was no surprise to her that so many students were eager to participate.

Michelle went first. "Right here is the bench," she began, pointing to the base ten blocks she used to model the problem. "Here's the two people. On each bench two people are sitting. There's two people on each bench."

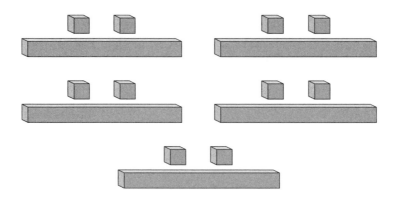

"Does everyone see what Michelle did?" Alison asked the class. "How did you find out the answer, Michelle?"

"I counted them all," Michelle responded. Alison waited to see if Michelle would tell the class *how* she counted. When no further explanation was forthcoming, Alison helped by asking questions and providing some sentence starters.

"What did you do first?" Alison asked. "First I . . ."

"First I made the five benches," Michelle began.

"Next I . . . ," Alison prompted.

"Next I put two people on each bench," Michelle continued. "Then I counted by twos."

Alison directed Michelle to point to her materials as the students counted aloud by twos: "Two, four, six, eight, ten."

When Michelle was finished, Alison led the class in a round of applause. Jennifer, a student with beginning English language skills, was next to share.

"They were on the benches eating the snack," she began, pointing to the materials on the rug in front of her. "They're eating. And, um, and they were separately. There were two on the bench. I counted the people. They were eating."

Recognizing that Jennifer was having some difficulty, Alison asked her a question designed for a beginning English learner. "Can you point to the objects that are the people?" This question was suited for a beginning English learner because it required Jennifer to show, not explain. Alison is conscious of the ways in which she can tailor her questions to students' language levels.

Michelle pointed to the two plastic spiders on each bench.

"So you counted the spiders for people?" Alison clarified. "Two on each bench?" Michelle nodded.

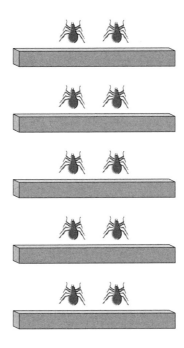

"Count and see how many people there are," Alison directed. Pointing to the spiders, Michelle counted aloud, one by one, until she arrived at the correct answer of ten.

After two more students finished sharing their solution strategies, the warm-up for math class was over. Alison directed the students to put their materials away, and she then proceeded with the math lesson for the day.

Devoting Math Time to Word Problems

Sometimes word problems are the main focus of math time in Alison's class, rather than just a warm-up. On another day, the students were again gathered on the rug, listening to Alison present a word problem orally.

Yareli has 10 treats for her puppies. She has two puppies.
How many treats does each puppy get to make it fair?

"Do you know what dog treats are?" Alison asked the class.
"They're like snacks," Isela said.
"If dogs are good, you give them treats," Chris added.
Alison then held up a little doggie biscuit that she had brought from home to show the students.

To retell the problem, Alison decided not to have the students use partner talk. This time, Alison asked three students to retell the story. She gave each volunteer lots of think time before he or she shared. Mei Ling, a student with intermediate fluency whose native language is Vietnamese, was one of the three students who retold the problem.

"Yureli got ten snacks for her two puppies," she began. "And how many, how many snacks does she need to give her puppies to make it fair?"

"How many treats does she need to give *each* dog?" Alison repeated, emphasizing *each*. As much as possible, Alison either paraphrases or rephrases students' ideas, or she asks the students to rephrase other students' ideas. Paraphrasing or rephrasing is beneficial in several ways. It gives English learners another chance to understand an idea; it provides an opportunity to practice producing language; and it gives the teacher a chance to model correct usage of grammar and syntax.

Unlike the first day, when students solved the word problem at the rug, Alison dismissed the class to their seats to work. To transition them from the rug, she distributed to each student a sheet of paper on which was written the word problem and a reminder to show their work using numbers, pictures, or manipulatives. In addition, there were three sets of number choices that students could use when solving the problem:

(10, 2)   *(12, 3)*   *(15, 2)*

These number choices allowed Alison to differentiate instruction. For example, dividing ten dog treats into two groups would be easier than dividing fifteen into two groups. Students were able to self-regulate, with some assistance from the teacher, and choose which numbers were appropriate for them. Having three different number pairs also gives early finishers further practice.

As the students worked, Alison circulated. When students work on word problems, Alison sees her role mainly as an observer, keeping track of the strategies students are using. Sometimes she'll choose a few children who have solved the problem in different ways to share in the upcoming whole-class discussion; this gives all students access to a variety of ways to solve word problems.

Sharing Strategies

To transition to the rug, Alison had the students leave their manipulatives at their tables and only bring their papers. Once they were all seated in a circle on the rug, Alison asked the students to raise their hands if they solved the first problem: ten dog treats for two dogs. Then, on the count of three, Alison directed the class to say the answer to the problem aloud.

Yareli, a student with advanced fluency in English, volunteered first to share her thinking.

"I already knew that five plus five equals ten," Yareli said. "I could break apart the ten to give five treats to one puppy and five to the other. So each puppy gets five."

Yareli is a good example of an English learner who has some strong language skills that help her explain her thinking clearly and accurately. Her explanation served as an excellent model for others. (See Figure 8–7.)

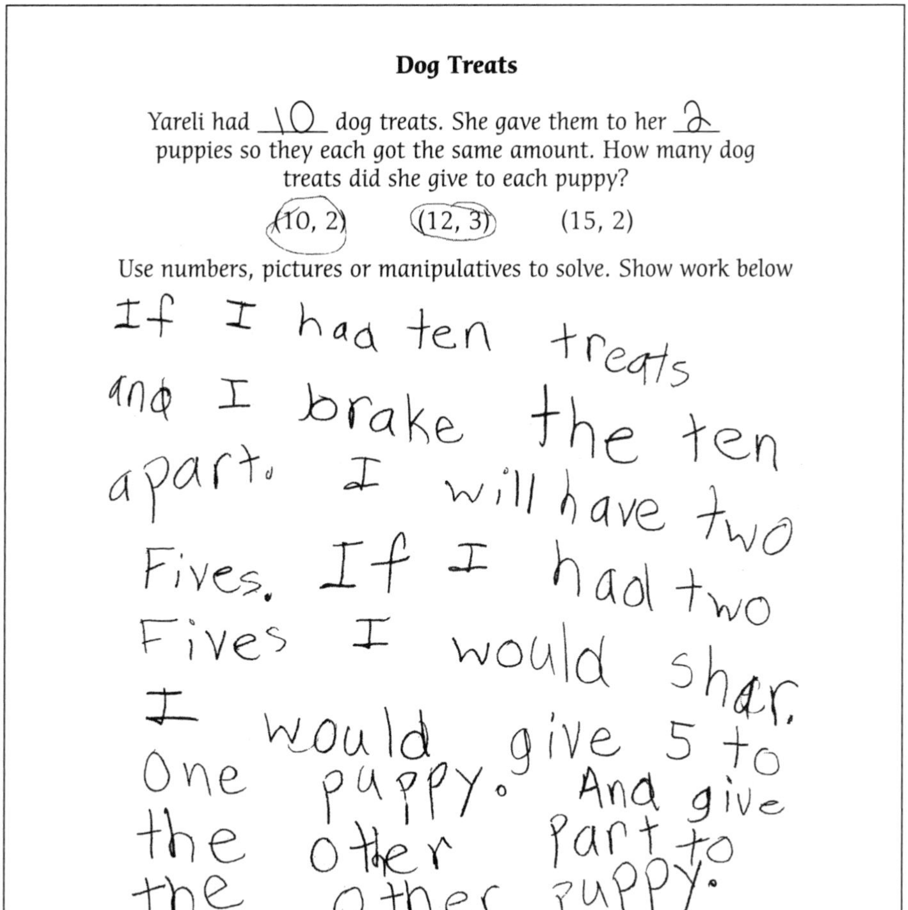

Dog Treats

Yareli had __10__ dog treats. She gave them to her __2__ puppies so they each got the same amount. How many dog treats did she give to each puppy?

(10, 2)   (12, 3)   (15, 2)

Use numbers, pictures or manipulatives to solve. Show work below

If I had ten treats and I brake the ten apart. I will have two Fives. If I had two Fives I would shar. I would give 5 to One puppy. And give the other part to the other puppy.

FIGURE 8–7. Yareli is an example of an English learner with strong language skills.

Vanessa, another student with advanced fluency, went next. She had worked on the problem with three dogs and twelve dog treats.

"I had three puppies," Vanessa began. "I mean Yareli had three puppies. Then I got—then I found that twelve is an even number and then I got the cubes."

Alison gave Vanessa a bag of interlocking cubes so that she could show the class what she did.

Continuing, Vanessa said, "I gave one to this puppy, one to this puppy, and one to this." Vanessa was making three groups, or puppies, and divvying the cubes or treats to each puppy, one at a time.

"And then two and two and two," she said, placing more cubes so that there were two cubes in each group. "And then three and three and three and then four and four and four."

Having the cubes was extremely helpful to Vanessa; the cubes seemed to facilitate her explanation and served as a conversation piece.

"Can someone tell us what Vanessa just said?" Alison asked the class.

Thomas, a student with intermediate fluency in English whose native language is Vietnamese, rephrased Vanessa's explanation. As he spoke, Alison made his thinking visible to the class by drawing a picture on chart paper.

"There's three dogs," Thomas said. Alison quickly sketched three dogs on chart paper.

"And she had twelve treats," he continued. Alison then drew twelve circles below the dogs.

"Yareli gave each dog a treat," Thomas continued. Alison drew a line from each dog to one treat.

"Then she gave each dog another treat and she kept doing that till each dog got four treats."

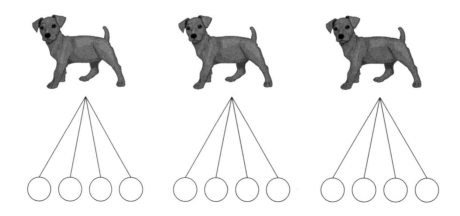

Supporting English Language Learners in Math Class, Grades K–2

"Vanessa's strategy reminds me of the other day when Kerin brought in gummy bears to share with the class," Alison said. "So that everyone got the same amount, Kerin passed one gummy bear to each student and then another to each person so that it was fair, remember?"

Students nodded their heads in agreement. Alison is always trying to find ways to connect the mathematics that students are learning to their experiences in everyday life. These connections help build and cement understanding for all students, particularly English language learners.

Figures 8–8 and 8–9 show how two other students solved this problem.

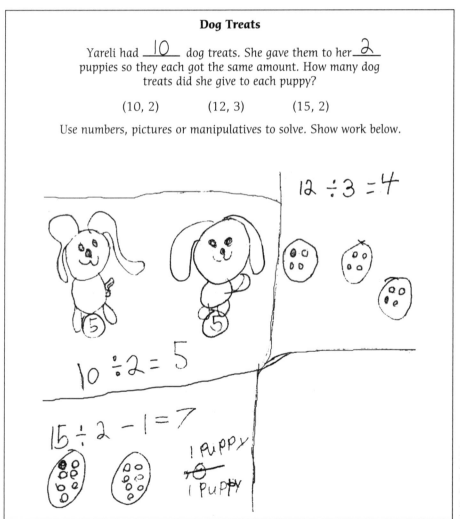

FIGURE 8-8. Jessica was able to use division to solve the problems.

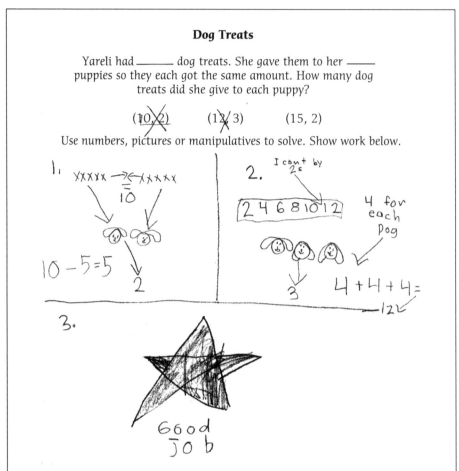

Dog Treats

Yareli had _____ dog treats. She gave them to her _____ puppies so they each got the same amount. How many dog treats did she give to each puppy?

(10, 2)   (12, 3)   (15, 2)

Use numbers, pictures or manipulatives to solve. Show work below.

1. XXXXX →←XXXXX
   10
   10 − 5 = 5
   2

2. I count by 2s
   | 2 4 6 8 10 12 | 4 for each Dog
   3   4 + 4 + 4 = 12

3.
   Good Job

FIGURE 8-9. Thomas clearly showed his thinking using words, numbers, and pictures.

Removing the Barrier of Language

Story problems are just math problems with words. But for a student who is learning a second (or third) language, words in that new language can create a barrier to understanding. By explicitly teaching English in math class, teachers can help remove the roadblock that often prevents English language learners from making sense of and therefore solving math word problems. In fact, the challenges that vocabulary, grammar, and syntax pose to English learners can become English language development opportunities in math class. Amy, Sharon, and Alison's teaching examples prove this.

The teachers in these three classrooms use strategies that clarify language and make math content accessible. They make language visible through the use of realia, playacting, pictures, gestures, and manipulatives. They help students grasp difficult words by using synonyms. They repeat, rephrase, and have students retell so that English learners have many chances to comprehend. They build in time for their students to talk *and* they provide support for the talk with prompts and frames. These teachers hold high expectations for all of their students, including their ELLs. And most importantly, Amy, Sharon, and Alison allow their students to make sense of mathematics in their own way, once the barrier of language is lifted.

9 How to Modify Math Lessons to Support English Language Learners

Education for English language learners (ELLs) in American classrooms has improved greatly over the last few decades as research has provided educators with strategies that make instruction more comprehensible. Teachers use visuals and manipulatives, capitalizing on the concrete nature of mathematics, to show students the subject matter content instead of just telling them about it. They simplify language so that ELLs can understand explanations more easily. They highlight key terms and often provide students with math journals or math vocabulary walls to be used as reference tools. All of this effort goes a long way toward making the teacher's lesson comprehensible to students whose native language is not English.

Comprehension is not a one-way street, however. It is not enough that the information is presented concretely and clearly. In order for a student to learn the concept being presented, he needs to interact with the information and make connections between what is already known and what is being learned. The learner then needs to test his new understandings by explaining what was learned. All of these steps in the learning process—interacting with new knowledge, making connections, and testing understandings— happen through language. Moreover, they require that the students produce language. It is at this point that the process often breaks down for the English language learner. Without adequate linguistic support, an English language learner cannot articulate his thinking. And if the concept happens to be a completely new one, the ELL's very *thinking* is compromised because humans use language to think.

Providing appropriate linguistic support involves consideration of each English language learner's proficiency level in English. Most English language development tests place students in one of various levels, typically described as beginning, intermediate, and advanced. Within each level there is still a range of ability, and since students are generally tested only once a year, the accuracy of the score decreases as time passes and as the student progresses. Typically speaking, however, students at the beginning level respond nonverbally. They can still participate in tasks that demonstrate comprehension, such as identifying, matching, and categorizing, but only with strong visual and manipulative support. Students at the intermediate level can describe, explain, define, retell, summarize, and compare and contrast. While they need less physical support in terms of visual aides, they need grammatical support as they struggle to find the right words and arrange them in coherent sentences. ELLs at the advanced level can perform all of the higher-level functions that a native speaker can perform, giving opinions, justifying answers, negotiating, debating, persuading, and so on, but they need the fine-tuning necessary for them to be considered fluent speakers of English. While the specifics of language development may not be foremost in the mind of the teacher during a math lesson, it is during content instruction that the student is learning new information and has an authentic need to communicate her understandings. It is also during content instruction that the teacher has a need to assess student learning. Language must be the vehicle, and not the roadblock, for both of these goals.

This book contains a collection of carefully crafted lessons from different strands of mathematics. The lessons were selected because of their appropriateness across grade levels and because they introduce new concepts in each of the strands. They were designed with all of the different language proficiency levels in mind. While we hope these lessons allow your English language learners to experience more success in math, you, the classroom teacher, are our true audience for this book. We hope these lessons serve as models for modifying the key lessons you present throughout the course of the academic year. This chapter is designed to help you think about how to approach math instruction in order to best support students who are learning the English language and math simultaneously.

Selecting Math Lessons for Modification

Obviously, we are not suggesting that teachers rewrite their entire math curriculum. While new information is presented in most lessons, the information generally builds on concepts previously introduced. Once English language learners have a solid understanding of the basic concepts, adding new information is a less onerous process. Providing students with support in the development of the necessary language during introductory lessons will allow them to interact with the information, make the necessary connections, and test their thinking as the instruction continues. Some lessons provoke more thinking and communication than others. Therefore, we suggest you select the key lessons that introduce new concepts in each strand, chapter, or unit of study and lessons that require students to use new vocabulary and language structures to think and communicate. Modifying these lessons will ensure that ELLs benefit from your subsequent instruction.

Whether or not you decide to try adapting a lesson in the style we are modeling, the sample lessons will help you think about the role of language in the math classroom. Although it may be easy to find satisfaction in the deceptive nods that English language learners give when asked if they understand a concept, it is much more reliable and informative to provide students with the opportunity and the language to articulate their understandings. The way teachers question ELLs can also affect the students' level of oral participation. If you ask questions with students' English proficiency levels in mind, they will be more likely to respond in a way that both solidifies their own understanding and allows you to assess their learning. The lesson vignettes in this book both address and provide examples of level-appropriate questioning. Additionally, focusing on the intricacies of the English language can help a teacher monitor whether or not the instruction is comprehensible. Multiple-meaning words and homophones can cause confusion for English language learners. A simple clarification of the intended meaning of a term can help them keep pace with the lesson. A list of multiple-meaning words used in mathematics is provided in the Appendix.

Modifying the Math Lesson

The lessons in this book have two goals, a math goal and a language goal. The math goal must be determined first; the language goal supports students' understanding of the math goal. Once you have identified what math content you are going to teach, think about what students would be able to say if they had met the math goal. For example, if the math goal involves learning about squares, once students had met that goal they would be able to *describe* squares and perhaps *compare and contrast* them with other geometric figures. If the math goal is that students solve a subtraction problem using an effective strategy that makes sense to them, then they would be able to *describe the sequence* of steps they used for solving the problem once they had met the goal. If the math goal states that students will learn about repeating patterns, then they would need to use language to *predict* which colored cube will come next in the series. Each of these three math goals—learning about shapes, solving subtraction problems, and understanding repeating patterns—has a logical language goal (or goals) that accompanies it. In these cases the language goals are describing, comparing and contrasting, sequencing, and predicting.

Native English-speaking children are able to perform these language functions to articulate their math understanding when prompted with questions like "What do you know about squares?" "What are your steps for solving a subtraction problem?" and "What do you predict will come next in the pattern?" English language learners may understand the content of the lesson, but their inexperience with the language can keep them from articulating what they know. It is also possible that their struggles with the language of instruction lead them to partial or inaccurate understandings of the content. Until they verbalize their understandings, what they have learned or not learned remains a mystery to the teacher and may even be unclear to the students themselves. Choosing a language goal, or language function, that matches the math content goal makes the learning more observable to all.

Choosing the language goal is made easier by using the function chart in Figure 9–1. It lists twelve common functions of language as applied to the study of mathematics.

Determining Language Functions and Creating Sentence Frames

As there are purposes, or applications, for the various strands in mathematics, so are there purposes, or functions, for language. We use language to describe, to compare, to contrast, to predict, to categorize. Whether we are describing or categorizing in science, reading, social studies, or math, the sentence structure we use will be the same. For example, we might say that a butterfly has four stages in its

Language Functions and Sentence Frames		
Function	**Beginning**	**Intermediate and Advanced**
Describing Nouns	A ____ has ____. A ____ is ____	A ____ has ____, ____, and ____. A ____ is ____, ____, and ____.
Examples	A *square* has *four sides.*	A *triangle* has *three sides, three vertices,* and *no curves.*
Categorizing	A ____ is a ____.	A ____ is a ____ because ____. A ____ is not a ____ because ____.
Examples	*Two* is an *even number.*	*Four* is an even number because *it can be divided into two equal groups. Four* is not an *odd number* because *nothing is left over when you make two groups.*
Describing Location	The ____ is next to the ____.	The ____ is next to the ____ and below the ____.
Examples	The *square* is next to the *triangle.*	The *square* is next to the *triangle* and below the *circle.*
Compare/ Contrast	A ____ has ____. A ____ is ____.	A ____ has ____, but a ____ has ____. ____ and ____ both have ____.
Examples	This *group* has *three blocks.*	This *group* has *three blocks,* but *that group* has *five blocks.* Both *groups* have *blocks.*
Summarize	A ____ has ____ and ____. ____ is ____ and ____.	____ always have ____. Some ____ are ____ and some are ____.
Examples	The *class* has *9 boys* and *11 girls.*	The *class* always has *twenty students.* Some *students* are *absent* and some are *present.*
Sequence	First, ____. Second, ____.	First ____, and then ____.
Examples	First, *I counted the red blocks.* Second, *I counted the blue blocks.*	First, *I put the blocks in groups of ten,* and then *I counted them.*
Giving and Following Directions	Point to the ____. Draw a ____.	Put the ____ below the ____. Draw a ____ around the ____ and a ____ above the ____.
Examples	Draw a *square.*	Put the *square* below the *triangle.*
Hypothesizing	N/A	If ____, then ____ will ____.
Examples	N/A	If *I put thirty-six* blocks in groups of ten, then *I* will *have some blocks left over.*

FIGURE 9-1.
Language
functions
and sentence
frames.

Language Functions and Sentence Frames		
Function	**Beginning**	**Intermediate and Advanced**
Predicting	The ___ will have ___. The ___ will be ___.	I predict that ___ will ___. I predict that ___ will ___ because ___ .
Examples	*The next block* will be *green*.	I predict that *the next block* will be *green*. I predict that *the next block* will be *green* because *the pattern goes green-red-green-red*.
Making Inferences	N/A	I can infer that ___. I know that ___ because ___.
Examples	N/A	*I can infer that I need to add the numbers*. *I know that I need to add the numbers because it asks how many altogether*.
Drawing Conclusions	N/A	I can conclude that ___ .
Examples	N/A	*I can conclude that there are six blocks left over*.
Cause and Effect	The ___ is ___.	___ because ___.
Examples	*The answer is a bigger number*.	*The answer is a bigger number because we added two numbers together*.

FIGURE 9-1. *(Continued)*

life cycle, the main character in a story has a problem to solve, a community has firefighters, merchants, and teachers, or a triangle has three sides. Each one of those describing statements uses the same basic sentence structure: _____ *has* _____. We call this structure a *sentence frame*. Consider the function of cause and effect: If we provide a plant with water, soil, and sunlight, it will grow; if the character in the story finds a comfortable bed, she will fall asleep in it; if a farmer plants a food crop, he will be able to sell it at the market; if I divide the pizza in eighths, the four of us will get two pieces each. The frame is the same in all cases: *If* _____, _____ *will* _____. This is also true for other skills like categorizing. In science you might say that lizards, snakes, and crocodiles are reptiles because they are cold-blooded and lay eggs. In reading you would say Cinderella and Goldilocks are protagonists because they are the leading characters in literary works. In social studies certain individuals are heroes because they made a difference in their communities. And in math certain figures are squares because they have four equal sides and four right angles. In every case the language is supported by the same frame: _____ is a _____ because _____. These basic sentence structures can be powerful tools in the hands of students learning the English language. When structured appropriately, they are flexible enough to be useful in a variety of contexts. These frames allow such students to use the key vocabulary terms and put together complete thoughts, thoughts that can be connected, confirmed, rejected, revised, and understood.

Remembering that the students' language proficiency must be taken into account in order to provide the support that nudges students to the next level, teachers can design frames to create sentences that are increasingly more sophisticated. For example, if students are comparing and contrasting numbers or shapes in math, different English language learners will be ready to use language to think about and discuss their learning at various levels. Students with beginning levels of proficiency will be describing the numbers or shapes before they can compare and contrast them. They might use the frame _____ has _____ to express ideas like "A square has four sides" and "A triangle has three sides." Such a limited frame would not service intermediate or advanced students. They are ready to compare with frames like _____ has _____, but _____ has _____, composing sentences like "A square has four sides, but a triangle has three sides." The goal of the frames is twofold: to provide ELLs the linguistic support they need to learn about and demonstrate their knowledge of the math content while pushing their English language abilities to the next level of proficiency. The frames also provide practical applications for the language students are learning during their English language development lessons.

While the frames may seem abstract outside the context of the math lesson, English language learners almost immediately see the usefulness of them because they help students out with the hard parts of the language. Before students are asked to use a sentence frame, they learn key vocabulary terms that they can place in the frame to begin to talk about their learning. Frames are also introduced with familiar math concepts before they are used with new information. For instance, students might describe common classroom objects using the descriptive frames before they describe triangles. Once students understand the concept of the frame, they often try to use frames above their proficiency level, realizing that the frames allow them to produce much more complicated sentences than they would ordinarily use. The goal is not to create a fill-in-the-blank sentence that has correct and incorrect answers; rather, the frames should provide a scaffold that English language learners can use to construct and discuss their thoughts.

While the students' language development levels matter a great deal when designing frames, their ability to read is less of a concern. Of course, literate children are able to read the various frames and choose between them independently. Still, students with emergent levels of literacy make just as much use of the frames in an auditory manner. Preliterate students listen as the teacher uses a frame to hear how to structure their verbal responses. The teacher writes the frame or frames out and posts them to make sure she incorporates and models the vocabulary and syntax that will help students articulate their thinking. All of the language and teacher talk that goes into presenting a new concept overwhelms many ELLs, especially those with beginning levels of proficiency. When the teacher introduces and models the frame aloud, it helps the language learner focus on the key vocabulary and learn how to structure some words around the key vocabulary in order to say something about the concept. This very careful and intentional use of speech by the teacher is what promotes oral language development, an important building block for literacy.

Refer to the chart in Figure 9–1 to determine the language function that students will need to perform in order to articulate the particular math knowledge you want them to learn. Will they be describing geometric shapes, categorizing numbers, comparing the lengths of objects, predicting the next object in a repeating pattern, or drawing conclusions about a set of data?

Once you have determined the function, choose frames that meet the linguistic needs of your students, whether they are beginning, intermediate, or advanced. Mold the frames to fit the grade level and the particular lesson. Consider the number of blanks necessary for your frame. For example, *A square has* _____ is a helpful frame for very young students, but *A* _____ *has* _____ might be more appropriate for older students. Another important factor in creating frames is verb tense. Do you want students to articulate their thinking in the past, present, future, or conditional tense? When predicting, the future tense is the most logical because you are making educated guesses about an event that has not yet happened. When asking students to sequence the steps they used to solve a math word problem, setting the frames in the past tense makes more sense. The conditional tense is ideal for hypothesizing: "If I counted by twos, would the answer be the same?" Think about whether the subject of the frame is singular or plural. The answer to this question affects the article and the verb in the frame you choose. If students are describing a singular object, say a rectangle, they will need a frame designed for a single object: *A _____ has _____.* If students are describing a series of numbers, they will need a frame designed for multiple items: *_____, _____, and _____ have _____.* Once you have determined your frame, try it out yourself several times to make sure it is flexible enough to articulate many different examples. If slight modifications are necessary, using both singular and plural subjects, for example, be prepared to modify the frame as the students are using it.

Determining Key Vocabulary

Most math books now include a set of key terms for each lesson. This is a great place to start determining what words English language learners will need to know, but it is by no means an exhaustive list. Since math knowledge is cumulative, students who have spent less time learning in English may not know the previously taught terms that are the foundation for a particular lesson. In addition to content terms, consider some of the language in your frames that may be unfamiliar. For example, if you are asking students to predict, do they know what *predict* means? Are there any other terms that you want students to be able to use during the lesson that you haven't heard them use with confidence in general conversation? If a term is not in the students' oral vocabulary, directly teaching it might be a good idea.

Once you have determined the key vocabulary for the lesson, give some thought as to when to teach each term. Some of the words must be taught at the beginning of the lesson in order for students to follow along. Other words will not appear until partway through the lesson, and it may be more logical to teach them at that time. For example, teaching the word *cents* would be important to start off a lesson on the different types of coins. Teaching the words *penny, nickel, dime,* and *quarter* may not be necessary until the time when each coin is introduced. The students will better retain the meaning of the words once they have an actual need for them. Anticipating that need and providing the vocabulary at that moment will have the most impact on student learning.

Designing a Minilesson to Introduce the Mathematical Language

Learning math and language at the same time is a cognitively demanding endeavor. In order to support English language learners, design a minilesson that will allow students to try out the frames on familiar math material before they are faced with the academic demands of the grade-level lesson. The plans in this book provide models for such lessons. When we wanted students to learn to sort and categorize and articulate their categories, we began with a group of familiar objects, colored pencils, that varied in only one characteristic, color. When we wanted students to discuss sums in a card game, we began with 2 + 2. Allowing students to practice the frames with familiar concepts helps them internalize the frames, builds their confidence in volunteering answers, and prepares them to be successful during the math lesson.

Building in Opportunities for Talk

Language goals, sentence frames, and key vocabulary are useful to the students only if they have opportunities to talk during the lesson. All of these linguistic supports are meant to scaffold students' learning during instruction as well as allow them to showcase their learning after instruction. Arguably the most important role of the sentence frames is to help the students formulate their thinking as they are learning the math content. That thinking must occur throughout the lesson in order for the students to keep pace with the instruction.

Building in opportunities for structured and guided talk throughout the lesson will promote both thinking and learning. These opportunities for student talk will also allow the teacher to redirect students if misconceptions or confusions arise. Consider using any or all of the following strategies for facilitating student talk in your lesson.

Think, Pair, Share

After each meaningful chunk of instruction, provide students with time to think about what they have learned, pair up with a partner to discuss their ideas, and then share their ideas with the class. Scaffold all three of these activities by posting, explaining, modeling, and encouraging the use of the sentence frames.

Repeating and Rewording

During the presentation of a lesson, students are exposed to many important concepts. Often these concepts build on one another to achieve the math goal of the lesson. Achievement of that math goal can be improved if teachers hold students responsible for each important chunk of learning throughout the lesson. One way to accomplish this is to ask students to either repeat or reword key concepts as they are presented. While repeating may not seem like a high-level task, it is much more active than simply listening to the concepts as they are presented. Rewording key information encourages students to express a new concept in their own language, a language we know they understand. Students can repeat or reword statements made by the teacher or by other students. The teacher can also repeat or reword statements made by students in order to emphasize or question information.

Partner Work and Group Work

When directing students to explore with manipulatives, practice a skill, solve problems, conduct an experiment, draw a figure, discuss a chart, or compare numbers, have students work with a partner. Working with a partner creates the need for communication. Communication requires the thoughtful use of language. This is yet another opportunity for students to use the sentence frames and the key vocabulary to build their content knowledge and their language ability.

Supportive Questioning

Probably the most common way for teachers to invite student participation in a lesson is through questioning. While inquiring and checking for understanding are natural parts of teaching, simply asking questions may not elicit the desired participation from all English language learners. Students with advanced proficiency levels in English may respond to questions, as would any native English speaker, yet students with intermediate and beginning proficiency levels may need more support in order to produce a response. When asked a question such as "What steps did you use to solve the problem?" students with intermediate and beginning proficiency levels must produce so much language just to structure their answer (language to sequence their steps, past-tense verbs, math vocabulary) that they might choose not to answer at all.

A teacher can provide support, however, to elicit responses and improve the participation of students with lower levels of English proficiency. When questioning beginning-level students, ask a question or provide a prompt that requires a physical response ("Point to the square." "Touch the even number.") or a question with a yes-or-no answer ("Is this a rectangle?"). When asking short-answer questions, build the answers into the questions for additional support: "Is this a circle or a square?" "Is the number odd or even?" "Should we add or subtract?"

Students with intermediate levels of proficiency in English need less support to understand and respond to questions from the teacher, but carefully crafted questions can improve the quality of both their responses and their English. For example, instead of asking an intermediate-level student, "What do you predict will be next?" you might phrase your question this way: "What color do you predict the next cube will be?" The second question models the structure of a well-crafted answer: "I predict the next cube will be red." Compare that with the response more likely from the first question: "Red."

Questioning students lets teachers know what students have learned. Answering questions lets students test, confirm, or modify their own understandings. None of these goals can be met unless the questions are structured in a way that produces a response from the students. In addition to improving student participation, thoughtful questions can improve the quality of the students' responses.

Explaining Thinking

When teaching the lesson, make sure to prompt students to explain their thinking. When a student provides either a correct or an incorrect answer to a question, the more important information is how the student arrived at that answer. The correct answer may have been a lucky guess. It may also have been the result of good mathematical reasoning and problem solving that could serve as an example for other students. There is no way of knowing unless we ask students to explain their thinking. Likewise, an incorrect answer may have been the result of a careless mistake or it may represent complete confusion on the part of the student. Asking students to explain their thinking makes the learning process more transparent. Students with beginning levels of proficiency in English may not yet have the language necessary to explain their thinking. Providing manipulatives or visuals so that such students can *show* their thinking can provide insight into their learning.

Writing About Thinking

English language development involves four domains: listening, speaking, reading, and writing. Once students can verbalize their ideas about the math content using the sentence frames and the key vocabulary, they are ready to stretch to the next level and write down their ideas. Their writing is scaffolded by the frames as well as by the talk.

How We Develop Lessons

When designing lessons for English language learners, we follow a few important steps. The process is recursive, of course, as we return to particular sections of each lesson to revise our plan and make it as coherent as possible. Following is a sample of how we designed one particular lesson, *From Rockets to Polygons* (see Chapter 3).

Identify a math goal.

We selected the math goal of identifying, naming, and describing common two-dimensional geometric shapes and their attributes because it is a concept that is introduced in primary elementary grades and then built upon in future grades. This important concept is the type of basic knowledge that English language learners will need in order to be successful in their future math studies.

Choose a language goal that serves the math goal.

Knowing that students would be identifying, naming, and describing common shapes and their attributes, we determined that the language goal would be for students to describe objects.

Determine key vocabulary.

Many of the terms we introduced in this lesson came straight from the adopted math curriculum, such as *triangle*, *rectangle*, *square*, and *sides*. We chose other words to stretch the math vocabulary of the students: *vertex* and *vertices*, *angles*, and *polygons*.

Design sentence frames.

This lesson was designed for a primary classroom that consisted of native English-speaking students and English language learners at the beginning, intermediate, and advanced levels. We used the function chart to guide us as we created frames that would support students in this particular lesson. We decided that the beginning-level students could describe shapes by using these frames: *A _____ has _____ and It has _____*. We wanted the intermediate and advanced students to use more language, so we made their frames more grammatically demanding: *A _____ has _____, _____, and _____; My shape has _____; I built my shape with a _____ and a _____; and It looks like a _____*. The first three frames require students to use attributes to describe their geometric shapes. The final frame requires more advanced thinking as it asks the students to describe a shape by likening it to a concrete object. We practiced using these frames with the content from the lesson until we were satisfied that they were usable and supportive.

Design a minilesson to introduce the academic language.

Before we asked students to dive into the content of describing complex polygons, we designed a small activity in which they used the sentence frames we would be working with to describe a more familiar shape, a square. We also introduced most of the key vocabulary at this point so that students were equipped with useful language before they took the plunge into new learning. We saved the term *polygons* for later on in the lesson.

Build in opportunities for talk.

We began providing students with opportunities to talk in the minilesson. We asked them to speak with a partner at least three times before we introduced the frames. Once the frames were taught, we gave the students additional opportunities to practice them in the whole group and with partners. We also asked students to respond chorally many times throughout the minilesson and the main lesson in order to make sure all students were participating and practicing the language they were acquiring to help them articulate their new math learning.

The main lesson involved each student constructing and then describing her own polygon. Each student then described the shape to her partner, to the teacher, and then to all of her classmates in the whole group.

Design a writing prompt.

We ended the lesson by asking students to write about their shapes because writing extends and cements student thinking. Students could use the sentence frames to help spell words as well as to structure their responses. The extensive oral practice during the lesson prepared the students to write about their new learning.

Now You Try It

Identify a math goal.

Select a math goal for your lesson. Remember that you are looking for key concepts that build foundational knowledge, promote critical thinking, and/or involve an extensive use of language.

Choose a language goal that serves the math goal.

Once you have selected an appropriate math lesson for modification, decide what language students will need to articulate their learning. Think about what they will say throughout the lesson to demonstrate that they are learning the concept. What language function will they need to perform? Will they need to describe, categorize, compare, contrast, summarize, sequence, give directions, hypothesize, predict, make inferences, draw conclusions, or establish cause and effect?

Determine the key vocabulary.

What math terms will be introduced in this lesson? What previously introduced terms or everyday words are still unfamiliar to the ELLs in your class? What multiple-meaning words will appear in the lesson? Are there any other essential words that might cause confusion? List these terms and decide when in the lesson you will introduce each one.

Design sentence frames for multiple proficiency levels.

Use the "Language Functions and Sentence Frames" chart (Figure 9–1) to find sample frames that match the language function you chose. Work with the frames until they fit the needs of your lesson. Determine what verb tense would sound most natural. Decide how many blanks to include in each frame and where to put them. Design frames that will fit the various English proficiency levels represented in your class and will allow students to verbalize the key lesson concepts. Record the frames on chart paper or sentence strips.

Design a minilesson to introduce the language.

Once you have created your sentence frames, design a brief lesson in which the students can practice the frames with familiar math content. For example, if the students will be comparing large numbers, have them practice using the frames with smaller, less cumbersome numbers. If students will be summarizing the steps used to solve complicated computational problems, plan a lesson in which they use the sentence frames to summarize the steps used to solve a more basic problem. Remember that the goal of this minilesson is to familiarize the students with the sentence frames so that during the main lesson they can devote their thinking to the math content.

Build in opportunities for talk.

Beginning with the minilesson and continuing throughout the main math lesson, build in opportunities for students to talk to one another and to you about their learning. These opportunities should include discussions that build background and allow students to make connections to what they already know about the topic, exploratory talk that encourages students to hypothesize or make predictions about the new concept, clarifying conversations in which students explain what they think they understand about the new concept, and concluding conversations in which students solidify their new knowledge. Also, spend time crafting questions to ensure the participation of students with different proficiency levels. Refer to the suggestions in "Building in Opportunities for Talk" (see page 169) to ensure there is a variety of activities that will keep students engaged and participating.

Design a writing prompt.

While talk allows students to explore their knowledge in a relatively nonthreatening manner, it does not necessarily provide the teacher with information on each individual student's learning. In order to assess what students have learned both mathematically and linguistically from the lesson, design an open-ended question or prompt and ask students to commit their ideas to paper at the conclusion of the lesson. Refer students to the sentence frames for support with this activity. Encourage students to draw what they learned if they are not yet comfortable expressing their ideas in writing.

The template in Figure 9–2 is designed to help you capture all of the information you have been considering while designing your lesson. This is the type of document you could save for math instruction in future years, share with colleagues who are looking for ways to support their English language learners, or even modify to use with other subject areas like science and social studies.

Lesson Template

Math Goal:

_____

_____

Language Goal:

_____

_____

Key Vocabulary:

_____   _____   _____

_____   _____   _____

_____   _____   _____

_____   _____   _____

Materials:

_____   _____   _____

_____   _____   _____

Sentence Frames to Support Language Goal:

    Beginning: _____
    Intermediate: _____
    Advanced: _____

Activity Directions for the Minilesson (including opportunities to talk):

1.
2.
3.

Activity Directions for the Main Lesson (including opportunities to talk):

1.
2.
3.
4.
5.

Writing Prompt:

_____

_____

FIGURE 9-2.
Lesson
template.

Reflecting on the Modifications

When we wrote the math lessons detailed in this book, it took the three of us working together to design the lessons and then several test runs to revise them. We observed each other's lessons and took notes on the teaching and the learning, and then we met to debrief each lesson. It was reflecting on our planning and on our teaching that led us to many of the insights we have shared in this book. We learned what Farrell (2003) meant by saying that experience alone is not as important as reflecting on that experience.

After teaching a math lesson you have modified to better support your English language learners, take the time to reflect on how success-ful the lesson was. Did the ELLs in your class meet the math goal? Did they meet the language goal? Did they participate more than they normally do in math lessons? Were the frames you created appropriate for the lesson? Did you use too many frames or too few? What changes would have made the lesson more successful?

The work of modifying math lessons in order to not only make the lesson comprehensible but also provide language support to help English learners think about new concepts, experiment with their knowledge, and solidify their understanding is not easy. This is the type of work, however, that allows English language learners to fully participate in their learning community and fully benefit from your teaching.

10 Frequently Asked Questions

1. The ideas presented in this book just seem like good teaching. Why is it targeted for English language learners (ELLs)?

While it is true that all learners will benefit from the strategies presented in this book, they are essential for ELLs to have access to the core math curriculum. Without the use of explicit vocabulary instruction, visual aids, and opportunities to communicate during math lessons, ELLs would have difficulty understanding the material presented, be it verbal or written. This could create huge gaps or misunderstandings in the math concepts presented. Try to imagine yourself learning new content about teaching in a second language. It would be essential for the instructor to provide scaffolds for you to make sense of the material he was presenting. Again, while the native speakers may also benefit from the scaffolding, the support would be essential for *your* learning.

A second, even more compelling reason this book is targeted for ELLs is the focus on the development of the English language needed to participate fully in the math lessons. The implementation of the sentence frames provides ELLs with linguistic support so they can communicate mathematically and deepen their learning. This, in turn, provides us with opportunities for assessment and helps us make pivotal instructional decisions for our students.

2. Do the strategies in this book work for all ELLs regardless of their native language?

The strategies in this book will be effective for helping all ELLs, whatever their native language. Most teachers find that students who have strong oral language skills in their primary language have an easier time acquiring a second language, in this case, English. All ELLs benefit from direct, explicit instruction in English; simply being in an English environment is not enough. Hence, the strategies in this book will help your students learn math content and acquire English, regardless of their primary language.

3. What if I have only a few ELLs in my class and they are all at different language levels? Will this affect my native English-speaking students?

This is a common concern, as many teachers are in this exact situation. We have found that it is very appropriate to teach these lessons to the whole group and that the majority of students benefit from the additional attention to English. Since many children in the primary grades are still developing their oral language skills in conjunction with their literacy skills, the frames offer all students opportunities for growth. For example, native English-speaking students tend to use the intermediate and advanced frames, which have more complex academic language than they are used to using. Although they may have been able to explain their mathematical thinking without the support of the frames, native English speakers are now acquiring a more sophisticated way of doing so. For ELLs at different proficiency levels, teachers can regulate the use of the different frames. Higher-achieving students can self-regulate their use of the different frames, which is why all students are introduced to and practice all of the frames regardless of their level of English proficiency. However, in some classrooms where the makeup of students is extremely diverse (high achievers, ELLs, resource), small groups may be the best way to teach the minilessons or the entire lesson.

4. I have a student in my class who barely speaks any English. What can I do to support the student?

It is not uncommon to have students in your classroom who are at the very beginning stages of learning English. Students often come directly from their home countries speaking little or no English. This can create quite a challenge for a teacher trying to ensure that the newcomers have equal access to content. Here is a list of strategies that we have found to be extremely helpful in working with students at this stage:

◆ Use visuals and manipulatives to model problem solving and allow students to work with them during math. In the *Junk Sorting* lesson (see Chapter 7), students use concrete materials to categorize objects according to certain criteria. In addition, teachers can use visuals instead of only words in order to describe the categories for sorting (e.g., use colors to sort by color; a piece of wood, metal, or other material to sort by material). The manipulatives also provide students with a nonverbal way to demonstrate their understanding. By showing rather than telling, students provide us an opportunity for some assessment of their understanding even though we may not have a verbal explanation to accompany it.

✦ Prompts that require nonverbal responses are another way to include beginning ELLs in math lessons. By carefully crafting our questions to allow students to point to, hold up, or show us a response, we encourage them to participate more in the lessons, thereby giving us opportunities to assess learning. As students acquire some of the simpler terms in English, we can then begin to ask questions that require one-word responses such as *yes* or *no*, *red*, or *four*.

✦ If the circumstances allow, consider seating the beginning student near another student who has some proficiency in the same language as the newcomer. This can be tricky when working with very young children as they tend to be self-centered, but providing a newcomer with a buddy who shares her primary language can allow the newcomer some access to the curriculum that she may otherwise not have at all. As teachers, we have to establish the balance between burdening bilingual students with being "teachers" and fostering their own development as learners.

✦ Using sentence frames, creating a safe context for using English, and allowing students to practice English after direct instruction will also all contribute to helping newcomers begin the transition to an English classroom environment.

5. My English language learners seem to struggle more in math than my other students. Should I adjust my expectations for these students?

The adjustments need to occur in the presentation of material and not in what is expected of students. It may seem that ELLs struggle more in math compared with your native English speakers. This, however, does not indicate that they are in any way less capable than other students or that the expectations for them should be lowered. What you are witnessing may be the barrier that language has created, which does not permit ELLs to demonstrate their understanding of material.

Language difficulties may be masking the good mathematical thinking that ELLs are capable of and could possibly express in their primary language.

What we need to do as educators is adjust our instruction to find out what our students know and value the experiences they have had. Once we know more about our students, then we can design instruction to make sure we are providing them with an equitable education and allowing them access to the entire curriculum that native English-speaking students receive on a daily basis. It is our professional obligation to modify our lessons so that all students meet grade-level standards.

6. What is academic language and how is it different from social language?

Academic language is known as the language used in schools. But what exactly does that mean? It is the language that we use in formal learning environments connected to specific subject matter. For example, we may direct students to *summarize* a story, make a *causal statement* about the Civil War, or *draw conclusions* about a scientific experiment. These cognitive functions are correlated to a certain type of language structure that students need to understand, whether material is presented orally or in text, and must be able to produce orally or in writing. In addition to the text structure, word order (syntax) and vocabulary (topic-specific terms related to a subject) are also part of academic language. Acquiring academic language is key to success in schools and access to higher education.

In regard to the math lessons in this book, the language goals listed for each lesson are the language functions that we identified as the key cognitive tasks that students will be doing in the lessons. For example, when students participate in *Cubes in a Tube* (Chapter 6), the academic language they will need to know to be able to fully participate in the lesson is language for describing and predicting patterns, such as *I predict that the next cube will be _____* or *The pattern is _____*, and specific vocabulary terms such as *pattern*, *repeating*, color words, and *predict*. Academic language is usually content dense and often highly decontextualized, which increases the chance for difficulty in understanding and applying it.

In contrast, social language is easier to acquire as it is often used in everyday interactions surrounding common activities and topics. We don't always need specific terminology when speaking in social situations since we can usually refer to the topic at hand, such as the show on TV or the game on the playground. We also can use other ways to communicate besides language, such as gestures, phrases, and colloquial words, in order to participate in discussions. In addition, because of the frequency with which we interact in informal situations, there are many opportunities to practice the language of socializing or everyday activities. Many times our ELLs seem very adept with English, but we should always be checking to see whether their fluency is with the social use of English or the demands of academic English.

7. Some of my ELLs are really good at computation. Math is the only time that they can be successful without having to speak English. Why the emphasis on talking during math class?

Providing time for productive talk in math class can improve students' computation abilities. Being good at computation requires the kind of flexibility in thinking that enables a student to choose an efficient strategy for a particular problem to yield a correct answer. In order for students to become flexible problem solvers, they must be aware that numerous strategies for finding an answer may exist. By participating in mathematical discussions, students become aware of a variety of computation strategies and get a chance to develop their English language skills at the same time.

In addition, many concepts in math involve noncomputational, critical thinking. Since teachers instruct using language and students learn and think through language, devoting time to discussions during math instruction is essential for developing mathematical knowledge. Finally, without providing a forum for students to discuss their mathematical thinking, we might make incorrect assumptions about the learning that is occurring during math time. To be effective math instructors, we must assess thinking and learning, and language is the medium through which we do that.

8. This book is for kindergarten through second grade. Some of my students are emergent readers or in the early stages of mathematical development. Will the lessons, as written, work for all three grades?

Given the wide range of reading proficiency and overall development between kindergarten and second grade, we make some recommendations that may be more appropriate for different groups of students. First, we offer alternatives for the lessons for different grade levels. For example, in Chapter 4, we provide three different game options: *Trade*

Up for a Nickel, Trade Up for a Dime, and *Race for a Quarter.* You should select the lesson that will best match where your students are in their mathematical development. In addition, we suggest teaching the lessons in small groups to make them more manageable and comprehensible. With other lessons we present a two-day format and suggest that the first day be used with younger students and the first and second day with older ones. Finally, we recognize that not all students will be readers, so for classrooms with emergent readers, we emphasize the use of the sentence frames in an oral context so students don't have to read the frames in order to engage in mathematical discussions.

The idea of this book is to demonstrate how to support ELLs in math and to provide some examples in the various math strands for the primary grades. We suggest drawing on these lessons as guides, using the ones in the book as highly structured activities that you can try out and implement immediately with your students. Then, after experimenting with the lessons and strategies, you can begin to apply the strategies in the book to modify your own math lessons. Moreover, you know your students and your math curriculum best, so you will be the most adept in deciding if the lesson content is appropriate to your group of students and in determining the amount of adjustments you'll have to make.

9. I noticed that a lot of the lessons have minilessons, but some don't. Why is that?

The purpose of the minilessons prior to the math lessons is to introduce and practice the vocabulary and sentence structures students will need to fully participate in the math lessons. Keeping in mind the purpose, we can think about the minilessons in different ways according to the nature of the lessons. There may be formal minilessons, minilessons embedded as part of a game format, or no minilesson at all.

The lesson *From Rockets to Polygons* (Chapter 3) provides a good example of when to use a formal minilesson. This lesson was taught in a first-grade classroom where the students were already familiar with basic geometric shapes; therefore, the minilesson was the perfect venue to introduce the geometric vocabulary and the sentence frames critical to full engagement in the polygon lesson. Using squares as the familiar content in the minilesson, we were able to focus the learning on the English language that students would need in the math lesson to describe polygons. When you are able to explicitly teach new vocabulary and sentence structures with a familiar math topic, that is the time to use a formal minilesson.

Another way to include a minilesson is to embed the instruction of vocabulary and sentence structures into a game format. During the introduction of a game, you explicitly teach the specific words and language structures students will use during the game. For example, in the lesson *Capture and Double Capture* (Chapter 2), Christine simultaneously taught the students how to play the game while having them practice the vocabulary and sentence frames as part of the game itself. There was no reason to have a separate minilesson with other content, as the game directions provided an adequate and meaningful context for teaching and practicing the sentence frames and vocabulary.

Finally, in some lessons there are no minilessons. Minilessons are designed to use prior knowledge of math content in order to teach the new language structures, and there are times when it is difficult to find a topic to connect to with which the majority of the students are familiar. In *Trade Up for a Nickel* (Chapter 4), taught in a kindergarten class, the vocabulary surrounding money was new to many of the students. In addition, the math topic itself was part of the kindergarten curriculum; therefore, many students probably had little formal instruction with money before this lesson. For that reason, Kathy first tapped prior knowledge by asking students what they knew about money, and then she taught the vocabulary during the lesson and had students use the sentence frames chorally to describe the quantities of pennies and nickels and indicate when it was time to make a trade. The math content and language content were taught concurrently.

Although students come to school with many life experiences, those experiences might not always be the right ones for making connections to math content. It is essential to recognize and build upon the background of students, but it is just as important to distinguish the best times for doing so. In the case of *Trade Up for a Nickel*, a minilesson building on students' knowledge of money wouldn't have been as good a use of time as explicit instruction in language during the lesson itself.

10. I noticed in your lessons that you spend time practicing the sentence frames orally before beginning the math lessons. I'm worried about time. Is the oral practice really necessary?

One of the things that we know about teaching is that there never seems to be enough time for everything we would like to do in a day. Adding more to our day just seems impossible. We need to constantly scrutinize our schedules to make sure we are maximizing learning time for our students. In this case, we do need to make the time for oral language practice before jumping into a math lesson. If students do not get to practice the frames in the minilessons with content that is less cognitively demanding, they will not refer to them at all when they are engaged in the more taxing math lesson. Building in time for practice encourages students to use the academic language that will be required of them in the math lesson and gives them opportunities to receive feedback on that language. Once they feel some ownership of the language, they will be more likely to apply it later on. It is important that oral language practice has a meaningful purpose, and the minilessons provide that authentic setting to rehearse the new language while reviewing or introducing key mathematical ideas. The time invested in oral language practice prior to and during the lesson will improve student learning, thereby saving time that would have been spent reteaching the math concepts later on.

11. Do students get confused when there are too many sentence frames? How many sentence frames should I present at a time?

Students absolutely can become confused with too many sentence frames and frames that are not presented well. Ideally we would suggest one sentence frame for the key mathematical concept of the lesson, differentiated for the levels in your class. To visually differentiate the frames, we color-code them so that it is easy for teachers to distinguish one from another. Older students also respond well to the color-coding, as it allows them to self-monitor the language they use by experimenting with different levels and determining which ones they are comfortable with and which frames allow them to challenge themselves.

In kindergarten through second grade, even native English speakers are still developing their oral language skills. Therefore, in order to best match the proficiency levels of the students, we introduced only two levels of frames. We have a beginning frame and an intermediate and advanced frame for most of the lessons. We found that combining the last two levels was sufficient in supporting students to express their mathematical thinking. It is important to remember as well that the frames are intended as support for students and are not meant to stifle those individuals who have alternative, yet correct, ways of expressing their thinking.

Appendix

Multiple-Meaning Words in Mathematics

acute
altitude
base
change
chord
closed
combination
composite
coordinate
count
degree
difference
digit
edge
even
expression
face
factor
fair
figure
foot
formula
function
identity
improper
inequality

inscribe
intersection
irrational
key
left
mass
mean
median
multiple
negative
net
obtuse
odd
open
operation
origin
period
plane
plot
point
power
prime
product
proper
property
range

rational
ray
reflection
relative
right
root
round
ruler
scale
segment
set
side
similar
slide
solution
space
sum
table
term
times
translation
union
unit
value
volume
yard

Blackline Masters

Trade Up for a Nickel Game Board

1 penny = 1 ¢

1 nickel = 5 ¢

From *Supporting English Language Learners in Math Class, Grades K–2* by Rusty Bresser, Kathy Melanese, and Christine Sphar. © 2009 Math Solutions Publications.

Trade Up for a Nickel Amount Cards

1¢	2¢	3¢	1¢
2¢	3¢	1¢	2¢
3¢	1¢	2¢	3¢
1¢	2¢	3¢	1¢
2¢	3¢	1¢	2¢

Trade Up for a Dime Game Board

1 penny = 1¢

1 dime = 10¢

Trade Up for a Dime Amount Cards

1¢	2¢	3¢	4¢
5¢	1¢	2¢	3¢
4¢	5¢	1¢	2¢
3¢	4¢	5¢	1¢
2¢	3¢	4¢	5¢

Race for a Quarter Rules

You need: 1 zip-top bag of coins

        1 die

1.   Take turns. On your turn, roll the die. The number on the die tells you how many pennies to take.

2.   Exchange coins if you can.

3.   Give the die to your partner.

4.   Play until a player trades for a quarter.

Notes:

1.   You may exchange only when you have the die.

2.   Watch to be sure you agree with what your partner does.

3.   When you finish, count to check the number of coins in the bag. It should have 30 pennies, 10 nickels, 10 dimes, and 1 quarter.

From *Supporting English Language Learners in Math Class, Grades K–2* by Rusty Bresser, Kathy Melanese, and Christine Sphar. © 2009 Math Solutions Publications.

1-100 Chart

1	2	3	4	5	6	7	8	9	10
11	12	13	14	15	16	17	18	19	20
21	22	23	24	25	26	27	28	29	30
31	32	33	34	35	36	37	38	39	40
41	42	43	44	45	46	47	48	49	50
51	52	53	54	55	56	57	58	59	60
61	62	63	64	65	66	67	68	69	70
71	72	73	74	75	76	77	78	79	80
81	82	83	84	85	86	87	88	89	90
91	92	93	94	95	96	97	98	99	100

From *Supporting English Language Learners in Math Class, Grades K–2* by Rusty Bresser, Kathy Melanese, and Christine Sphar. © 2009 Math Solutions Publications.

References

Burningham, John. 2003. *Would You Rather . . . ?* New York: Chronicle Books.

California Department of Education Website. The Language Census Data, 2006–2007. www.cde.ca.gov.

Carrasquilo, Angela, and Philip Segan, ed. 1998. *The Teaching of Reading in Spanish to the Bilingual Student.* 2d ed. Mahwah, NJ: Lawrence Erlbaum.

Chapin, Suzanne H., and Art Johnson. 2006. *Math Matters: Understanding the Math You Teach, Grades K–8.* 2d ed. Sausalito, CA: Math Solutions Publications.

Chapin, Suzanne H., Catherine O'Connor, and Nancy Canavan Anderson. 2003. *Classroom Discussions: Using Math Talk to Help Students Learn, Grades 1–6.* Sausalito, CA: Math Solutions Publications.

Cobb, Paul, Ada Boutfi, Kay McClain, and Joy Whitenack. 1997. "Reflective Discourse and Collective Reflection." *Journal for Research in Mathematics Education* 28 (3): 258–77.

Cummins, Jim. 2004. "Supporting ESL Students in Learning the Language of Mathematics." In *Mathematics: Every Student Learns, Grade 1.* New York: Scott Foresman Addison Wesley.

Dutro, Susana, and California Reading and Literature Project. 2003. *A Focused Approach to Frontloading English Language Instruction for Houghton Mifflin Reading, K–6.* Santa Cruz, CA: ToucanEd.

Dutro, Susana, and Carrol Moran. 2003. "Rethinking English Language Instruction: An Architectural Approach." In *English Learners: Reaching the Highest Levels of English Literacy*, ed. Gilbert G. García (227–58). Newark, DE: International Reading Association.

Education Resource Organizations Directory. Wdcrobcolp01.ed.gov/Programs/EROD/org_list.cfm.

Farrell, Thomas S. C. 2003. *Reflective Practices in Action: 80 Reflection Breaks for Busy Teachers*. Thousand Oaks, CA: Corwin.

Fillmore, L. W., and Catherine E. Snow. 2000. "What Teachers Need to Know About Language." www.cal.org/ericll/teachers.pdf.

Full Option Science System (FOSS) Series. 1993. Berkeley: Lawrence Hall of Science, University of California.

García, Gilbert G., ed. 2003. *English Learners: Reaching the Highest Level of English Literacy*. Newark, DE: International Reading Association.

Garrison, Leslie. 1997. "Making the NCTM's Standards Work for Emergent English Speakers." *Teaching Children Mathematics* 4 (3): 132–38.

Hiebert, James, Thomas P. Carpenter, Elizabeth Fennema, Karen C. Fuson, Diana Wearne, and Hanlie Murray. 1997. *Making Sense: Teaching and Learning Mathematics with Understanding*. Portsmouth, NH: Heinemann.

Hiebert, James, and Diana Wearne. 1993. "Instructional Tasks, Classroom Discourse, and Students' Learning in Second-Grade Arithmetic." *American Educational Research Journal* 30 (2): 393–425.

Hill, Jane D., and Kathleen M. Flynn. 2006. *Classroom Instruction That Works with English Language Learners*. Alexandria, VA: Association of Supervision and Curriculum Development.

Holtzman, Caren. 1995. *A Quarter from the Tooth Fairy*. New York: Scholastic.

Honig, Bill, Linda Diamond, and Linda Gutlohn. 2007. *Teaching Reading Sourcebook*. Berkeley, CA: Consortium on Reading Excellence (CORE).

Khisty, Lena L. 1995. "Making Inequality: Issues of Language and Meanings in Mathematics Teaching with Hispanic Students." In *New Directions for Equity in Mathematics Education*, ed. Walter G. Secada, Elizabeth Fennema, and Linda B. Adajian (279–98). New York: Cambridge University Press.

Krashen, Stephen D., and Tracy D. Terrell. 1983. *The Natural Approach: Language Acquisition in the Classroom*. Hayward, CA: Alemany.

Kress, Jacqueline E. 1993. *The ESL Teacher's Book of Lists*. West Nyack, NY: Center for Applied Research in Education.

Lampert, Magdalene. 1990. "When the Problem Is Not the Question and the Solution Is Not the Answer: Mathematical Knowing and Teaching." *American Educational Research Journal* 27 (1): 29–63.

McLaughlin, B. 1985. *Second-Language Acquisition in Childhood: Vol. 2: School-Age Children*. 2d ed. Hillsdale, NJ: Lawrence Erlbaum.

National Assessment of Educational Progress (NAEP). 2007. http://nationsreportcard.gov/math_2007/m0015.asp

National Clearinghouse for English Language Acquisition. 2007. www.ncela.gwu.edu/policy/states/reports/statedata/2005LEP/GrowingLEP_0506.pdf.

National Council of Teachers of Mathematics (NCTM). 2000. *Principles and Standards for School Mathematics*. Reston, VA: NCTM.

Teachers of English to Speakers of Other Languages (TESOL). 2006. "Access the Latest Standards Documents." Accessed November 1, 2007. www.tesol.org/s_tesol/seccss.asp?CID=281&DID=1771.

U.S. Department of Education. 2000. "Getting Ready for College Early: A Handbook for Parents of Students in Middle and Junior High School Years." Accessed November 1, 2007. www.ed.gov/pubs/GettingReadyCollegeEarly/index.html.

Wood, Terry. 1999. "Creating a Context for Argument in Mathematics Class." *Journal for Research in Mathematics Education* 30 (2): 171–91.